Gospel Pilgrimage Stories

Jesus @ 2000

A Modern Translation + Paraphrase of Gospel Texts and Illustrations

DREW WILLARD

WESTBOW
PRESS®
A DIVISION OF THOMAS NELSON
& ZONDERVAN

WestBow Press books may be ordered through booksellers or by contacting:

WestBow Press
A Division of Thomas Nelson & Zondervan
1663 Liberty Drive
Bloomington, IN 47403
www.westbowpress.com
1 (866) 928-1240

ISBN: 978-1-5127-7722-2 (sc)
ISBN: 978-1-5127-7723-9 (e)

Library of Congress Control Number: 2017902960

Print information available on the last page.

WestBow Press rev. date: 3/10/2017

Introduction

This book is a companion to the storytelling project I did in the summer of 2007. It was a "Gospel Storytelling Pilgrimage" as I stopped to visit churches, mentors, family, and friends along my way to the 26th General Synod of the United Church of Christ — which was also celebrating its 50th anniversary. I drove up from Florida to Hartford, Connecticut for GS XXVI then on to Massachusetts and back through New York, Pennsylvania, and finally to Washington, DC. From there I took a nice Autotrain ride back home. There were 19 scheduled performances and at 7:00 pm each day, I presented a 45 minute Biblical storytelling program followed by discussion. These are Gospel stories I translated or paraphrased from the Greek, using inclusive language to unpack meaning. The use of capital letters is a reminder of how these texts were often written in ancient times. The drawings are my own and serve more like medieval illuminations rather than illustrations. "Jesus @ 2000" was the basic design for my entry into a national art contest. The top 50 were published — mine must've been 51st...

'Born of the Virgin Mary, Suffered under Pontius Pilate' — but what happened in between? As the Nicene Creed tried to come up with a definition about God that early Christians could all agree to, this also meant coming to terms with who was — and is, Christ Jesus. There were three parts to my original repertoire — The first being "The Prologue" about the beginnings of Jesus' ministry, a harmonization with stories from each of the Gospels. I have included the Sermon on the Mount here as a separate text which continues from the Beatitudes of the Gospel of Matthew. These teachings are the heart of what Jesus equipped his apostles with, to go out two by two, to mend the world torn apart by Roman oppression and lay the foundation for the 'beloved community'. I use this term from America's civil rights struggle as an inclusive alternative for the 'Kingdom' that is possible, 'on Earth as it is in Heaven'.

The second part is about a day in the life of Jesus — which happens to be a Sabbath. Think of a day in your life that was filled with so many things going on — a day filled with adventure and wonders, that not one more thing could have been added to it? I had such a day keeping up with newspaper reporter and mentor, Chris Farlekas. On one visit to see him at Middletown, NY, after supper at a local diner, I followed along to attend a book signing, see a Shakespearean play, do an interview, talk until the wee hours, wake to have a late breakfast at a place known for its grain muffins, take in a movie (he was the Times Herald Record's media critic), and go to a Christmas craft fair to interview the folks of a Ukrainian church — all within 24 hours, a typical day in the life of Chris Farlekas! Now, imagine what it would be like to follow Jesus of Nazareth around for a day — appropriately enough, on a "Sabbath".

The third part concludes with a Passion narrative intertwined with stories about Mary Magdalene and Samaritans — good and bad, as Jesus makes the journey to his destiny at Jerusalem — a glimpse to his strategy of radical hospitality to bring the Good News of God's love beyond the Middle East. I call this "a Lovesong to God" because of its principal theme about love — and as my tribute to the One Who loves and seeks to befriend us all.

Many of these stories have been told by me in an interfaith setting as an "Evening of Sacred Storytelling", allowing people of other faiths to encounter Jesus through the non-threatening occasion of just hearing a good story — even to meet Jesus as a friend. So, blessings to you in the reading and hearing of this interpretation of God's Word and may you one day write your own lovesong to God.

Drew Willard
Florida, 2016

Contents

The Prologue

The Jordan

Mark 1:1-11

Inspired by Mark 1:1-11

IN THE BEGINNING OF THE GOOD NEWS OF JESUS CHRIST,
    THE MESSIAH, THE SON OF GOD,
        THE ONE WHO DESCENDED FROM GOD,
    AS IT WAS ATTESTED TO BY ISAIAH THE PROPHET:
"LOOK HERE!
I AM SENDING OUT MY ANGEL TO CONFRONT YOU
    WHO WILL PAVE YOUR WAY.
A VOICE DECLARES IN THE WASTELAND,
    'PREPARE THE WAY OF "THE ONE WHO IS";
        MAKE THE PATH STRAIGHT
          FOR GOD'."

JOHN THE BAPTIST APPEARED IN THE WASTELAND
    AND HE ANNOUNCED A BAPTISM
        FOR THE CHANGING OF ONE'S HEART & MIND
IN ORDER TO FORGIVE
        AS WELL AS BE FORGIVEN OF SINS.

AND PEOPLE JOURNEYED OUT TO HIM
    FROM THE WHOLE REGION OF JUDEA,
        ESPECIALLY FROM JERUSALEM;
    AND THEY WERE BAPTIZED BY HIM
        IN THE WATERS OF THE JORDAN,
CONFESSING THEIR SELFISH THOUGHTS & DEEDS.

NOW, JOHN WAS CLOTHED WITH CAMEL'S HAIR
    AND GIRDED ABOUT THE WAIST
        WITH A LEATHER BELT;
    AND HE ATE LOCUSTS,
        AND HONEY FROM WILD BEES.

AND HE PUBLICLY PROCLAIMED,
    "AFTER ME COMES ONE WHO IS
        MORE POWERFUL THAN I,
THE THONG OF WHOSE SANDALS
        I AM NOT WORTHY TO STOOP DOWN & UNTIE.
I AM BAPTIZING YOU BY WATER ALONE,
        BUT HE WILL BAPTIZE YOU IN A GREAT SPIRIT OF HOLINESS."

AND THEN IN THOSE DAYS,
    JESUS CAME FROM NAZARETH OF THE GALILEE;
      AND WAS BAPTIZED BY JOHN IN THE JORDAN.
AND INSTANTLY, AS HE ASCENDED FROM THE WATERS,
    HE SAW A SPLITTING OPEN OF THE HEAVENS;
      AND THE GREAT SPIRIT LIKE A DOVE
        CAME DOWN TO HIM.
AND A VOICE CAME FROM THE OPEN HEAVENS:
    "YOU ARE THE ONE WHO COMES FROM ME.
      YOU ARE ONE WHO IS BELOVED;
        IN YOU I <u>DELIGHT</u>!"

The Wasteland

Luke 4:1-15, Matthew 4:4b

Inspired by Luke 4:1-15

RIGHT THEN,
      JESUS TURNED BACK FROM THE JORDAN
           AND WAS URGED ON BY THE GREAT SPIRIT
      INTO THE WASTELAND OF BEING TEMPTED BY…
      ONE'S OWN WORST ENEMY.

FOR FORTY DAYS & FORTY NIGHTS,
      JESUS DID NOT EAT ANYTHING;
           AND AT THE END OF IT,
                HE WAS RAVENOUS…

THEN, THE ENEMY SAID TO HIM,
      "IF YOU ARE A 'SON OF GOD',
           SPEAK TO SUCH AS THAT STONE
                SO THAT IT BECOMES BREAD."
BUT JESUS ANSWERED,
      "IT IS BECAUSE OF SUCH AS THIS THAT IT IS WRITTEN,
           'HUMANITY DOES NOT LIVE BY BREAD ALONE,
      (BUT BY EVERY WORD THAT GOD IS STILL SPEAKING')."

[Matthew 4:4b]

AND JESUS WAS LED UP TO BE SHOWN
      ALL THE NATIONS OF THE WORLD
           IN AN INSTANT;
      AND THE ENEMY SAID TO HIM,
      "TO YOU I WILL GIVE
           THE POWER OF THIS WHOLE DOMAIN
                AND ITS SPLENDOR;
      FOR IT WAS GIVEN OVER TO ME
           TO GIVE TO WHOEVER I WISH.
      HERE IS MY FOOT TO KISS,
           AND YOURS, WILL BE ALL THIS."

BUT JESUS ANSWERED,
      "IT IS WRITTEN,
           'YOU SHALL WORSHIP THE ONE WHO IS…
           YOUR GOD WHO ALONE IS
                WORTHY TO BE SERVED'."

AND JESUS WAS LED INTO JERUSALEM
     AND PLACED AT THE TOP OF THE TEMPLE;
        AND IT WAS SAID TO HIM,
   "IF YOU ARE A 'SON OF GOD',
       JUMP DOWN FROM HERE!
          FOR 'BECAUSE OF THIS IT IS WRITTEN':
       'GOD'S ANGELS ARE AROUND YOU
          TO PROTECT YOU'
           AND THIS,
       'YOU WILL BE BORNE UP SO THAT YOU WILL NOT
          EVEN BUMP YOURSELF AGAINST A STONE'."

BUT JESUS ANSWERED,
     "IT IS...SAID...
        STOP TEMPTING THE ONE WHO IS
          YOUR GOD!"

AND THE TEMPTATIONS STOPPED;
     SO THE ENEMY BACKED OFF TO TRY AGAIN...

BUT JESUS RETURNED
     IN THE POWER OF THE GREAT SPIRIT,
        THE LIFE-BREATH OF HOLINESS;
     AND HIS REPUTATION WENT OUT
        THROUGH THE WHOLE VICINITY;
     AND HE PREACHED IN THE SYNAGOGUES THERE
        AND WAS PRAISED BY EVERYONE.

The Galilee

John 1:43-51

Inspired by John 1:43-51

JESUS RESOLVED TO GO THROUGHOUT THE GALILEE
     AND HE HAPPENED TO FIND PHILLIP,
          AND SAID TO HIM,
     "FOLLOW ME!"
NOW PHILLIP WAS FROM BETHSAIDA,
     THE HOMETOWN OF ANDREW AND PETER THE ROCK –
          WHO IS SOMETIMES CALLED, 'ROCKY'…

PHILLIP HAPPENED TO FIND NATHANIEL AND SAID TO HIM,
     "THE ONE WHOM MOSES WROTE ABOUT IN THE LAW
          AND THE PROPHETS IN THEIR WRITINGS –
               WE HAVE STUMBLED UPON HIM!
          JESUS JOSEPHSON,
               FROM NAZARETH!"
NATHANIEL SAID,
     "NAZARETH! CAN ANYTHING WORTHWHILE
          COME FROM THERE?"
PHILLIP SAID TO HIM,
     "COME SEE FOR YOURSELF!"

JESUS SAW NATHANIEL COMING TOWARDS HIM
     AND SAID ABOUT HIM,
     "LOOK HERE! AN 'ISRAELITE'
          IN WHOM THERE IS NO TREACHERY!"

BUT NATHANIEL SAID TO HIM,
     "NOW HOW WOULD SOMEONE LIKE YOU
          KNOW ANYTHING ABOUT ME?'
JESUS ANSWERED HIM,
     "BEFORE PHILLIP CALLED YOU,
          YOU WERE 'UNDER THE FIG TREE';
               I SAW YOU."
NOW [WHATEVER IT WAS THAT HAPPENED
     'UNDER THE FIG TREE' MUST HAVE BEEN SOME CRISIS
          OF LOYALTY AND TRUTH BECAUSE…]
     NATHANIEL ANSWERED HIM,
     "O RABBI! YOU ARE THE SON OF GOD! YOU ARE A KING!
          YOU ARE AN ISRAELITE LIKE ONE OF US!"

BUT JESUS ANSWERED HIM,
"BECAUSE I SAID,
'I SAW YOU UNDER A FIG TREE',
DO YOU TRUST ME?
YOU WILL SEE GREATER THINGS
THAN THIS!
I TELL YOU THE TRUTH,
YOU WILL SEE THE HEAVENS
HAVING BEEN TORN OPEN
AND THE ANGELS OF GOD
ASCENDING AND DESCENDING
IN THE PRESENCE OF THE SON OF MAN –
THE TRUE HEIR OF HUMANITY!"

Nazareth

Luke 4:16-30

Inspired by Luke 4:16-30

AND JESUS CAME TO NAZARETH
    WHERE HE HAD BEEN BROUGHT UP.
AND AS IT WAS HIS HABIT ON THE SABBATH DAY,
    HE WENT TO SYNAGOGUE.
AND HE GOT UP TO READ PUBLICLY, AND WAS GIVEN
    THE SCROLL OF THE PROPHET ISAIAH;
        AND UNROLLING THE BOOK
    HE HAPPENED TO FIND THE PLACE
        WHERE 'IT IS WRITTEN':

    'THE SPIRIT OF THE ONE WHO IS GOD
        RESTS UPON ME TO ANOINT ME
            TO PREACH GOOD NEWS
                TO POOR PEOPLE;
    I AM SENT
        TO PROCLAIM AMNESTY
            FOR CAPTIVE PEOPLE
        AND THE RECOVERY OF INSIGHT
            FOR PROUD BLIND PEOPLE;
    I AM SENT
        TO HEAL IN ORDER TO FORGIVE;
        AND
        TO PROCLAIM A YEAR OF RECONCILIATION
            WITH THE ONE WHO IS GOD'."

AND ROLLING UP THE SCROLL
    TO GIVE BACK TO THE ATTENDANT, HE SAT DOWN.
AND THE EYES OF EVERYONE IN THE SYNAGOGUE
    WERE RIVETED UPON HIM.
AND HE BEGAN TO SAY TO THEM,
    "TODAY, THESE WORDS ARE FULFILLED
        AS YOU HEAR…"
BUT EVERYONE WAS COMPLEMENTING HIM
    AND AMAZED AT THE ELEGANT WORDS
        THAT PROCEEDED FROM…
            HIS MOUTH.
THEN 'THEY' SAID,
    "ISN'T THIS JOSEPH'S… SON?"

AND HE SAID TO THEM,
 "MORE THAN LIKELY
  YOU WILL QUOTE TO ME THIS PROVERB,
  'PHYSICIAN, HEAL THYSELF.'
 AND YOU WILL SAY,
  'WHAT WE HEARD YOU DID IN CAPERNAUM,
   DO HERE FOR YOUR OWN PEOPLE'.
 I TELL YOU THE TRUTH,
  NO PROPHET IS EVER 'POLITICALLY CORRECT'
  IN ONE'S OWN HOMETOWN.
 IN ALL HONESTY I SAY TO YOU,
  THERE WERE MANY 'WIDOWS' IN ISRAEL
   AT THE TIME OF ELIJAH,
  WHEN THERE WAS NO RAIN FOR 3 ½ YEARS
   BUT THERE WAS A TERRIBLE FAMINE
   THROUGHOUT THE LAND;
  YET HE WAS SENT TO NONE OF THEM
   EXCEPT A WOMAN WHO WAS WIDOWED
   OF ZAREPHATH, OF SIDON –
   OF LEBANON;
  AND THERE WERE MANY 'LEPERS' IN ISRAEL
   AT THE TIME OF ELISHA THE PROPHET,
   BUT NONE OF THEM WAS CLEANSED
  EXCEPT NAAMAN… OF SYRIA!'

ALL WHO HEARD THIS WERE OUTRAGED!
 THEY SEIZED HIM AND DRAGGED HIM
  OUT OF THE SYNAGOGUE
 TO THE VERY BROW OF THE CLIFF
  ON WHICH THE CITY WAS BUILT.
THEY MEANT TO THROW HIM HEAD-FIRST
 OVER THE SIDE!
BUT CUTTING THROUGH THEIR MIDST,
 JESUS GOT AWAY…

Cana

John 2:1-11

Inspired by John 2:1-11

THERE WAS A WEDDING IN CANA OF GALILEE;
    JESUS' MOTHER WAS THERE,
        JESUS ALSO WAS INVITED,
            ALONG WITH SOME OF HIS FRIENDS.

WHEN THEY RAN OUT OF WINE, HIS MOTHER SAID TO HIM,
    "THEY ARE OUT OF WINE…"
HE SAID TO HER,
    "AH WOMAN…MOTHER!
    WHAT DO YOU WANT ME TO DO ABOUT IT?
        IT DOESN'T SEEM TO BE THE TIME
            FOR ME TO DO THIS SORT OF THING…"

HIS MOTHER SAID TO THE SERVANTS THERE,
    "WHATEVER HE SAYS TO YOU,
        DO IT!"

NOW SIX CARVED STONE JARS WERE STANDING NEARBY,
    USED FOR THE JEWISH RITES OF PURIFICATION,
        EACH HOLDING BETWEEN 20 OR 30 GALLONS.
JESUS SAID TO THE SERVANTS,
    "FILL THE JARS WITH…WATER."
SO, THEY FILLED THEM UP.

AND HE SAID,
    "NOW, DRAW SOME OUT
        AND BRING IT TO THE MASTER OF CEREMONIES."
SO, THEY DID IT.

WHEN THE MASTER OF CEREMONIES TASTED THE WATER –
    NOW SUPPOSEDLY CHANGED TO WINE,
        AND DID NOT KNOW WHERE IT CAME FROM –
    THOUGH THE SERVANTS
        WHO DREW THE WATER KNEW,
    THE MASTER OF CEREMONIES SENT FOR THE BRIDEGROOM…

AND HE SAID TO HIM,
  "MOST PEOPLE SERVE THE GOOD WINE FIRST
    AND AFTER EVERYONE IS DRINKING A LOT,
     THEN THE CHEAP STUFF.
  BUT <u>YOU</u> ARE ONLY JUST NOW…
    STARTING TO SERVE THE BEST WINE?"

JESUS PERFORMED HIS FIRST SYMBOLIC ACT
  IN CANA OF THE GALILEE
    AND DEMONSTRATED HIS GLORIOUS…
  SENSE OF HUMOR!
AND HIS FRIENDS WERE LIKEWISE TRANSFORMED
  INTO DISCIPLES.

Capernaum

Mark 2:1-12

Inspired by Mark 2:1-12

AND JESUS RETURNED TO CAPERNAUM
    AFTER A FEW DAYS.
AND WHEN PEOPLE HEARD THAT HE WAS AT HOME,
    SO MANY WERE GATHERED THERE
        THAT IT WAS NOT POSSIBLE
    TO GET THROUGH THE DOOR.
AND HE WAS PREACHING THE WORD OF GOD –
    THE WAY TO LIVE TO THEM.

THEN, 'THEY' CAME,
    FOUR PEOPLE CARRYING A PARALYZED PERSON.
AND WHEN THEY COULD NOT REACH JESUS
    THROUGH THE CROWD,
        THEY GOT UP ON THE ROOF.
AND WHEN THEY HAD DUG DOWN AND TORN OPEN
    A HOLE BIG ENOUGH,
        THEY LET DOWN THE STRETCHER
    ON WHICH THE PARALYZED PERSON LAY.

WHEN JESUS SAW THEIR FAITH,
    HE SAID TO THIS PARALYZED PERSON,
    "MY DEAR, YOUR SINS ARE FORGIVEN."

NOW, SOME RELIGIOUS EXPERTS WERE SITTING THERE,
    DIALOGUING LIKE THIS AMONGST THEMSELVES;
    "WHAT IS THIS?"
        "THIS IS BLASPHEMY."
    "WHO CAN FORGIVE SINS,
        BUT GOD ALONE?"

RIGHT THEN, JESUS, PERCEIVING IN HIS SPIRIT,
    THAT THEY WERE DEBATING LIKE THIS,
        SAID TO THEM,
    "WHY DO THESE QUESTIONS ARISE IN YOUR HEARTS?
        WHICH IS EASIER TO SAY
            TO A PARALYZED PERSON?
        'YOUR SINS ARE FORGIVEN',
            OR PERHAPS, 'GET UP AND WALK'…
    BUT THAT YOU MAY KNOW THAT
        THE SON OF MAN, THE TRUE HEIR OF HUMANITY,
            HAS THE POWER ON EARTH TO FORGIVE SINS…"

HE SAID TO THE PARALYZED PERSON,
    "I AM TELLING YOU TO GET UP,
        PICK UP YOUR STRETCHER…
            AND GO ON HOME."

AND THAT PERSON GOT UP,
    PICKED UP HIS STRETCHER,
        & PRACTICALLY DANCED OUT THE FRONT DOOR!
SO, THAT THEY WERE ALL ASTONISHED, AND SAID,
    "PRAISE GOD! WE NEVER SAW ANYTHING LIKE THIS!
        PRAISE GOD!"

The Kingdom

Matthew 5:1-16

Inspired by Matthew 5:1-12

AND SEEING THE CROWDS,
    [JESUS] WENT UP THE MOUNTAIN.
AND HE SAT DOWN WHEN HIS DISCIPLES HAD CLIMBED UP
    AND WERE BEFORE HIM.
AND FROM HIS LIPS CAME THIS TEACHING…

"TO BE RIPENED ARE THOSE WHO ARE CHALLENGED BY
    POVERTY AND DISABILITY,
    FOR THEIRS IS THE BELOVED COMMUNITY OF HEAVEN.
TO BE RIPENED ARE THOSE WHO SUFFER,
    FOR THEY SHALL BE COMFORTED.
TO BE RIPENED ARE THOSE WHO ARE HUMBLED,
    FOR THEY SHALL WIN IT ALL IN THE END.
TO BE RIPENED ARE THOSE WHO HUNGER AND THIRST
    FOR JUSTICE, FOR THEY SHALL BE SATISFIED.
TO BE RIPENED ARE THOSE WHO ARE MERCIFUL,
    FOR THEY THEMSELVES SHALL RECEIVE MERCY.
TO BE RIPENED ARE THOSE WHO ARE PURE IN HEART,
    FOR THEY SHALL SEE GOD IN ACTION.
TO BE RIPENED ARE THOSE WHO ARE PEACE-BUILDERS,
    FOR THEY SHALL BE CALLED THE CHILDREN OF GOD.
TO BE RIPENED ARE THOSE WHO ARE PERSECUTED
    FOR THE SAKE OF JUSTICE, FOR THEIRS, TOO,
        IS THE BELOVED COMMUNITY OF HEAVEN.

AND TO BE RIPENED ARE THOSE OF YOU WHO WILL
    BE CURSED, PERSECUTED, AND ACCUSED
        OF ALL KINDS OF TERRIBLE THINGS –
    AH, FALSELY ON MY ACCOUNT.
REJOICE AND ANTICIPATE THE GREAT REWARD THAT
    AWAITS YOU IN THE HEAVENS
        FOR THE PROPHETS WERE ABUSED IN THE SAME WAY.

Inspired by Matthew 5:13-16

YOU ALL ARE THE SALT OF THE EARTH,
     BUT WHEN SEASONING BECOMES TASTELESS,
          WITH WHAT SHALL IT BE MADE SAVORY AGAIN?
WHY, IT IS GOOD FOR NOTHING… YET EVEN THEN
     IT CAN BE THROWN OUT ON SLIPPERY WALKWAYS.

YOU ALL ARE THE LIGHT OF THE WORLD;
     A CITY BUILT ON A HILL CANNOT BE HIDDEN.
NO ONE LIGHTS A LAMP AND PLACES IT UNDER A BASKET,
     BUT ON A LAMPSTAND, SHINING FORTH
          TO ALL THOSE IN THE HOUSE.

IN THIS WAY,
     YOUR LIGHT MUST SHINE FORTH
          IN THE SIGHT OF ALL HUMANITY
     THAT THEY MAY SEE YOUR GOOD WORKS AND PRAISE
          FOR YOUR BELOVED GUARDIAN
          WHO <u>IS</u> IN THE HEAVENS.

The 3 Point Sermon on the Mount

Matthew 5:17-7:29
a modern paraphrase based on
<u>The New Greek English Interlinear New Testament</u>
J.D. Douglas, ed. Tyndale House Publishers, Inc. [1990]

It actually works to say that Jesus' greatest teaching was a 3-point sermon!

❖ *You have heard that it was said, 'One Way',*
   but I say to you, 'God is still speaking.'

❖ *Don't pray, donate, or serve just for show,*
   because God is with you wherever you go.

❖ *Do unto others as you would have them do unto you – or else!*

You have heard that it was said, 'One Way',
but I say to you, 'God is still speaking.'

Inspired by Matthew 5:17-20

DO NOT ASSUME THAT I CAME TO UNDERMINE
    THE LAW AND THE PROPHETS.
I DID NOT COME TO UNDERMINE THEM,
    BUT TO AFFIRM THEM.
I AM TELLING YOU THE TRUTH,
    NEITHER HEAVEN & EARTH
        NOR THE LEAST STROKE OF ANY LETTER OF THE LAW
    WILL PASS AWAY BEFORE EVERYTHING THAT IS
        SUPPOSED TO HAPPEN, DOES.

THEREFORE,
WHOEVER MAKES A HABIT OF BREAKING THE LAW OF LOVE –
    THE LAW OF LOVING-KINDNESS
        AND CONVINCES OTHERS TO DO THE SAME,
    WILL HAVE LITTLE TO DO WITH
        THE BELOVED COMMUNITY OF HEAVEN.
BUT WHOEVER PRACTICES AS WELL AS PREACHES
    THE LAW OF LOVING-KINDNESS WILL BE CONSIDERED
        A GIANT IN THAT BELOVED COMMUNITY OF HEAVEN.

FOR I TELL YOU THAT UNLESS YOUR RIGHTEOUSNESS
    EXCEEDS THE LITERAL INTERPRETATIONS OF
        THE PHARISEES AND OTHER RELIGIOUS EXPERTS,
    YOU WILL NOT EVEN ENTER
        THE BELOVED COMMUNITY OF HEAVEN.

Inspired by Matthew 5:21-26

"YOU HEARD IT WAS SAID TO THE ANCIENT ONES,
    'THOU SHALT NOT MURDER' AND
        'MURDERERS WILL BE BROUGHT TO COURT'.
BUT I SAY TO YOU,
    ANYONE WHO FESTERS WITH ANGER
        AGAINST SOMEONE WILL BE BROUGHT TO COURT.
AND WHOEVER CALLS SOMEONE BY A DIRTY NAME
    WILL FIND THEMSELVES IN PRISON.
AND WHOEVER CASUALLY SLIGHTS SOMEONE
    IS ALREADY IN HELL.
SO, BEFORE YOU BRING AN OFFERING TO GOD
    WHILE YOU ARE NURSING A GRIEVANCE, LEAVE YOUR GIFT,
        RECONCILE YOURSELF WITH THAT PERSON,
    THEN RETURN TO PRESENT YOUR OFFERING.

IF YOU GET INTO A BUSINESS DISPUTE,
    BE ON GOOD TERMS WITH YOUR ANTAGONIST,
        OTHERWISE YOU MAY FIND YOURSELF IN COURT,
    AND THE JUDGE HANDING YOU OVER TO THE SHERIFF
        AND DOING TIME IN PRISON.
I AM TELLING YOU THE TRUTH,
    THE WORLD WON'T LET YOU GET AWAY
        WITHOUT PAYING OFF ALL THAT YOU OWE.

Inspired by Matthew 5:27-32

YOU HAVE HEARD IT SAID,
     'THOU SHALT NOT COMMIT ADULTERY'.
BUT I SAY TO YOU THAT ANYONE WHO
     LOOKS UPON A PERSON WITH LUST
        HAS ALREADY COMMITTED ADULTERY
     AGAINST THAT PERSON IN ONE'S HEART.

NOW, IF YOUR 'RIGHTEOUS' EYE CAUSES YOU TO SIN,
     TEAR IT AWAY… BY CASTING YOUR SIGHT DOWN.
FOR IT IS BETTER NOT TO BE A SPECTATOR
     THAN TO BECOME A SPECTACLE YOURSELF.

AND IF YOUR 'RIGHTEOUS' HAND CAUSES YOU TO SIN,
     PULL IT AWAY AND KEEP YOUR DISTANCE.
FOR IT WOULD BE BETTER TO
     KEEP YOUR HANDS TO YOURSELF
        THAN FOR OTHERS TO SEIZE YOU.

AND IT HAS BEEN SAID,
     'WHOEVER DIVORCES HIS WIFE,
        LET HIM BE AUTHORIZED TO DO SO.'
BUT I SAY TO YOU THAT,
     ANY <u>MAN</u> WHO DIVORCES HIS WIFE –
        EXCEPT FOR SEXUAL DISLOYALTY,
          PUTS THAT WOMAN AT RISK IN SOCIETY.
FOR THERE IS UNFAIR SOCIAL PRESSURE
     AGAINST A DIVORCED WOMAN IN THIS WORLD.

Inspired by Matthew 5:33-37

AGAIN, YOU HAVE HEARD IT WAS SAID TO THE ANCIENT ONES,
    'THOU SHALT NOT BREAK THY WORD', AND
        "THOU SHALT HONOR THY PLEDGE TO THE LORD.'
BUT I SAY TO YOU,
    DON'T MAKE PROMISES AT ALL.
NEITHER BY HEAVEN WHICH IS THE THRONE OF GOD,
    NOR BY EARTH WHICH IS THE FOOTSTOOL OF GOD,
NOT BY JERUSALEM THE CITY OF THE GREAT KING,
    NOR BY THE HAIRS OF YOUR OWN HEAD
        COULD YOU PRESUME TO PROMISE ANYTHING.
FOR IT IS NOT YOU IN THE FIRST PLACE
    WHO COULD TURN EVEN A BLACK HAIR, WHITE.

BUT SAY, 'YES' OR 'NO' ABOUT WHAT YOU <u>DID</u> DO;
    FOR BEYOND THIS, IT IS JUST QUIBBLING.

Inspired by Matthew 5:38-42

YOU HAVE HEARD THAT IT WAS SAID,

    'AN EYE FOR AN EYE AND A TOOTH FOR A TOOTH.'

BUT I SAY TO YOU,

    DON'T HIT YOUR ABUSER BACK – WITH VIOLENCE THAT IS...

IF SOMEONE BACKHANDS THE RIGHT SIDE OF YOUR FACE,

    TURN SO THEY'D HAVE TO STRIKE THE LEFT SIDE –

        AND RISK BEING GUILTY OF ASSAULT.

AND IF SOMEONE SUES YOU

    FOR THE SHIRT OFF YOUR BACK,

        EMBARRASS THEM WITH YOUR NAKEDNESS

    BY OFFERING YOUR CLOAK, TOO.

AND IF A ROMAN SOLDIER FORCES YOU

    TO CARRY HIS PACK FOR A MILE –

        GO TWO MILES AND MAKE A FRIEND.

ANYTIME SOMEONE ASKS YOU

    TO GIVE THEM SOMETHING,

        OR TO BORROW SOMETHING,

    DON'T TURN YOUR BACK ON THEM.

Inspired by Matthew 5:43-48

YOU HAVE HEARD THAT IT WAS SAID,
 'THOU SHALT LOVE THY NEIGHBOR' AND
  'THOU SHALT HATE THINE ENEMY.'
BUT I SAY TO YOU,
 LOVE YOUR ENEMIES AND
  PRAY FOR THOSE WHO MISTREAT YOU,
 SO THAT YOU MAY BECOME
  CHILDREN OF YOUR HEAVENLY GUARDIAN.
FOR GOD HAS MADE
 THE SUN TO SHINE UPON THE EVIL
  AND THE GOOD;
 THE RAIN TO FALL UPON THE JUST
  AND THE UNJUST.

SO, IF YOU LOVE THOSE WHO LOVE YOU,
 ISN'T THAT ITS OWN REWARD?
  EVEN THIEVES AND TRAITORS DO THIS.
AND IF YOU ONLY WELCOME THOSE WHO ARE LIKE YOU
 WHAT WOULD BE NOBLE ABOUT THAT?
  YET, ISN'T THAT WHAT EXTREMISTS DO?
INSTEAD, PERFECT YOURSELF IN THIS WAY –
 BY PRACTICING GOD'S PERFECT WAY
  OF LOVING-KINDNESS.

Don't pray, donate, or serve
just for show, because God is
with you wherever you go.

NOW, BE CAREFUL THAT YOUR RIGHTEOUSNESS
  IS NOT FOR SHOW TO WIN FAVOR FROM OTHERS.
OTHERWISE, YOU WILL HAVE NO REWARD
  FROM YOUR HEAVENLY GUARDIAN.
THEREFORE, WHENEVER YOU GIVE YOUR OFFERING
  DON'T TOOT YOUR OWN HORN
    AS THE HYPOCRITES DO TO GET ATTENTION
  IN THE SYNAGOGUES AND PUBLIC PLACES.
    I TELL YOU THEY HAVE THEIR REWARD.
INSTEAD, YOU SHOULD MAKE YOUR DONATIONS
  SO THAT YOUR LEFT SIDE DOESN'T INTERFERE
    WITH WHAT YOUR RIGHT SIDE IS DOING.
THOUGH YOU MAKE YOUR DONATION ANONYMOUSLY,
  YOUR HEAVENLY GUARDIAN WILL KNOW
    AND REWARD YOU.

AND WHENEVER YOU PRAY,
  DON'T BE LIKE THOSE HYPOCRITES WHO LOVE
    TO MAKE A BIG SHOW OF THEIR PRAYERS
  IN THE SYNAGOGUES AND PUBLIC PLACES
    FOR THE ATTENTION.
I TELL YOU THE TRUTH,
  THEY HAVE ALL THE REWARD THEY WILL GET.
BUT YOU CAN PRAY EVEN WHEN YOU ENTER AN EMPTY ROOM
  AND SHUT THE DOOR.
SO, PRAY IN SOLITUDE
  FOR YOUR HEAVENLY GUARDIAN WILL SEE
    AND REWARD YOU.

Inspired by Matthew 6:7-13

NOW IN YOUR PRAYERS,
     DON'T BABBLE ON AND ON LIKE EXTREMISTS DO.
FOR THEY THINK THAT THEIR ELABORATE REQUESTS
     WILL BE HEARD.
DON'T BE LIKE THEM,
     BECAUSE YOUR HEAVENLY GUARDIAN
          ALREADY KNOWS WHAT YOU NEED
     EVEN BEFORE YOU ASK.
SO, PRAY LIKE THIS…

     GUARDIAN OF US ALL,
          WHO IS IN HEAVEN,
     LET YOUR NAME
          BE RESPECTED.
     LET YOUR BELOVED COMMUNITY
          COME TO BE.
     LET YOUR DESIGN UNFOLD
          ON EARTH AS IN HEAVEN.
     GIVE US TODAY
          THE BREAD WE NEED AND
     FORGIVE US OUR FAILURES
          AS WE FORGIVE THOSE WHO FAIL US.
     AND DO NOT ABANDON US TO DISASTER,
          BUT RESCUE US FROM THE EVIL-DOER.

Inspired by Matthew 6:14-18

SO NOW, IF YOU FORGIVE OTHERS' TRANSGRESSIONS,
    SHOULDN'T YOUR HEAVENLY GUARDIAN
        ALSO FORGIVE YOU?
IT FOLLOWS THAT IF YOU DO NOT FORGIVE OTHERS,
    NEITHER SHOULD YOUR HEAVENLY GUARDIAN
        FORGIVE YOUR TRANSGRESSIONS.

AND WHENEVER YOU FAST,
    DON'T BE LIKE GLOOMY HYPOCRITES WHO GRIMACE
        TO MAKE A BIG SHOW OF THEIR PIETY.
I AM TELLING YOU THE TRUTH,
    THEY HAVE ALL THE REWARD THEY ARE GOING TO GET.
BUT WHEN YOU ARE FASTING,
    ANOINT YOUR HAIR AND WASH YOUR FACE
        SO NO ONE CAN TELL YOU ARE FASTING
    EXCEPT YOUR HEAVENLY GUARDIAN
        WHO KNOWS IN SECRET.
AND YOUR BELOVED GUARDIAN
    WHO CAN SEE YOU EVEN IN YOUR HIDING PLACE
        WILL REWARD YOU.

Inspired by Matthew 6:19-23

DO NOT PRESUME YOU CAN HIDE YOUR TREASURES
      ON EARTH WHERE MOTHS AND RUST DESTROY AND
          THIEVES CAN BREAK IN AND STEAL.
BUT STORE YOUR TREASURES IN HEAVEN
      WHERE MOTH AND RUST AND THIEF
          CANNOT TOUCH THEM.
FOR WHERE YOUR HEART IS,
      THAT IS WHERE YOUR TREASURE WILL BE.

THE EYE ILLUMINATES ONE'S PHYSICAL SELF;
      SO, IF YOUR EYE IS HEALTHY
          YOUR APPEARANCE WILL SHINE.
BUT IF YOUR EYE IS FOCUSED ON EVIL,
      YOUR OUTLOOK WILL BE GRIM.
FOR WHEN GLOOM INFORMS YOU INSTEAD OF LIGHT,
      HOW SINISTER WILL THAT GLOOM BE.

Inspired by Matthew 6:24-27

NO ONE IS ABLE TO SERVE TWO BOSSES;
      FOR YOU WILL HATE ONE AND LOVE THE OTHER,
            OR STAND BEHIND ONE YET DESPISE THE OTHER.
YOU ARE NOT ABLE TO SERVE BOTH
      GOD <u>AND</u> GREED.

THEREFORE I SAY TO YOU,
      DON'T BE ANXIOUS ABOUT LIFE –
            WHETHER OR NOT YOU SHALL EAT AND DRINK
      OR HAVE CLOTHES TO WEAR.
ISN'T LIFE MORE THAN
      CONCERNS ABOUT FOOD AND CLOTHING?

DO YOU SEE HOW THE BIRDS OF THE SKY
      NEITHER SOW NOR REAP
            NOR GATHER FOOD INTO BARNS.
YET YOUR HEAVENLY GUARDIAN FEEDS THEM;
      AREN'T YOU MORE SIGNIFICANT THAN LITTLE BIRDS?
AND CAN ANY OF YOU EXTEND YOUR LIFE A DAY LONGER
      BY WORRYING ABOUT IT?

Inspired by Matthew 6:28-34

NOW, WHY WOULD YOU FRET ABOUT CLOTHES?
    THINK HOW FLOWERS GROWING IN A FIELD
        DON'T HAVE TO SPIN AND WEAVE.
    YET NOT EVEN SOLOMON WAS ARRAYED
        AS MAGNIFICENTLY AS THEY ARE.
THOUGH GOD HAS ADORNED SUCH WILDFLOWERS,
    WHICH ARE GROWING IN A FIELD TODAY
        YET TOMORROW ARE THROWN INTO AN OVEN,
WON'T GOD MORE GRANDLY ADORN YOU,
    O YE OF LITTLE FAITH?

THEREFORE, DON'T BE ANXIOUS, SAYING,
    'WHAT SHALL WE EAT? OR
        'WHAT SHALL WE DRINK?' OR
            'WHAT SHALL WE WEAR?'
AREN'T THESE THE THINGS
    THAT MATERIALISTS STRIVE FOR?
DON'T YOU THINK YOUR HEAVENLY GUARDIAN
    KNOWS THAT YOU NEED THESE THINGS?

BUT FIRST,
    SEARCH FOR THE KINGDOM OF THE BELOVED COMMUNITY
        AND THE RIGHTEOUS WAYS OF GOD,
    AND ALL THESE THINGS WILL TAKE CARE OF THEMSELVES.
SO, DON'T WORRY ABOUT TOMORROW –
    FOR TOMORROW WILL HAVE ITS OWN CONCERNS.
TODAY HAS CHALLENGES ENOUGH.

Do unto others as you
would have them do
unto you – or else!

Inspired by Matthew 7:1-5

DON'T JUDGE UNLESS YOU WANT TO BE JUDGED.

    FOR THE SCRUTINY WITH WHICH YOU SCRUTINIZE OTHERS

        WILL BE USED TO SCRUTINIZE YOU.

SO, THE MANUEVER ROOM YOU GIVE

    WILL BE THE SAME YOU GET.

AND WHY WOULD YOU NOTICE

    A SPECK IN SOMEONE ELSE'S EYE

        BUT IGNORE THE LOG IN YOUR OWN EYE?

YOU HYPOCRITE!

    TAKE THE LOG AWAY SO YOU CAN SEE CLEARLY ENOUGH

        TO HELP SOMEONE ELSE.

Inspired by Matthew 7:6-11

BUT DON'T GIVE SACRED THINGS TO HYENAS.
     DON'T TRUST YOUR TREASURES TO SWINE.
BECAUSE THEY WILL TRAMPLE THEM INTO THE MUD
     AND BREAK YOUR HEART.

ASK AND YOU WILL RECEIVE, SEEK AND YOU WILL FIND,
     KNOCK AND THE WAY WILL OPEN UP FOR YOU.
FOR EVERYONE WHO ASKS WILL RECEIVE;
     EVERYONE WHO SEEKS WILL FIND;
          EVERYONE WHO KNOCKS <u>WILL</u> FIND THEIR WAY.

NOW, IF YOUR CHILDREN ASKED FOR BREAD,
     WOULD ANY OF YOU GIVE THEM A STONE INSTEAD?
IF THEY ASKED FOR A FISH,
     WOULD YOU GIVE THEM A SNAKE?
EVEN IF YOU ALL WERE EVIL-DOERS,
     YOU WOULD STILL KNOW TO GIVE GOOD THINGS
          TO YOUR CHILDREN.
HOW MUCH MORE SO WILL YOUR HEAVENLY GUARDIAN
     GIVE GOOD THINGS TO YOU
          WHEN YOU ASK FOR THEM.

Inspired by Matthew 7:12-16a
THEREFORE,
ALL THAT YOU WISH OTHERS WOULD DO FOR YOU,
      YOU SHOULD DO SO FOR THEM.
FOR THIS IS THE SUM OF
      THE LAW AND THE PROPHETS' TEACHING.

SO, ENTER THE NARROW GATE RATHER THAN
      THE WIDE AND EASY WAY THAT LEADS TO DISASTER –
            THOUGH THERE ARE MANY WHO CHOOSE IT.
OY, HOW NARROW THE GATE AND DIFFICULT THE ROAD
      THAT LEADS TO AUTHENTIC LIFE – AND HOW FEW FIND IT!

BEWARE OF THE FALSE PROPHETS
      WHO COME TO YOU IN SHEEP'S CLOTHING,
            BUT INSIDE ARE RAVENOUS WOLVES.
YOU WILL KNOW THEM
      BY THE OUTCOMES THEY PRODUCE.

Inspired by Matthew 7:16a-23

YOU DON'T GET GRAPES
      FROM THORNS AND THISTLES.
LIKEWISE, YOU EXPECT TASTY FRUIT FROM AN APPLE TREE
      AND NASTY FRUIT FROM A CRABAPPLE TREE.
A HEALTHY TREE DOESN'T PRODUCE
      ROTTEN FRUIT,
AND A ROTTEN TREE DOESN'T PRODUCE
      HEALTHY FRUIT.
AND ANY TREE THAT DOESN'T PRODUCE HEALTHY FRUIT
      WILL BE CUT DOWN AND THROWN INTO THE FIRE.
SO, YOU WILL KNOW THEM
      BY THE HARVEST THEY PRODUCE.

NOT ALL THOSE SAYING TO ME,
      'LORD! LORD!' WILL ENTER THE BELOVED COMMUNITY
           OF THE HEAVENLY KINGDOM.
IT WILL ONLY BE THOSE WHO DO THE WILL
      OF MY HEAVENLY GUARDIAN – WHICH IS TO LOVE.

MANY WILL SAY TO ME ON THAT SUNRISE TO ETERNITY,
      'LORD, LORD, DIDN'T WE PROPHESY IN YOUR NAME
           AND DIDN'T WE CAST OUT DEMONS IN YOUR NAME?
      AND DIDN'T WE DO MANY MIGHTY WORKS IN YOUR NAME?'
AND THEN, I WILL DECLARE,
      'YOU NEVER REALLY KNEW ME.
           BEGONE, YOU LAWLESS OPPORTUNISTS!'

Inspired by Matthew 7:24-27

SO NOW,
EVERYONE WHO HEARS MY WORDS AND FOLLOWS THEM
      WILL BE CONSIDERED LIKE THE WISE PERSON
            WHO BUILT A HOUSE UPON A ROCK.
AND THE RAIN CAME DOWN,
      AND THE RIVER ROSE,
            AND THE WIND BLEW AGAINST THAT HOUSE.
BUT IT DIDN'T FALL BECAUSE ITS FOUNDATION
      WAS UPON THE ROCK.
AND ALL WHO LISTEN TO MY WORDS,
      BUT DON'T FOLLOW THEM,
            WILL BE LIKE THE FOOLISH PERSON
      WHO BUILT A HOUSE UPON SAND.
AND THE RAIN CAME DOWN,
      AND THE RIVER ROSE,
            AND THE WIND BLEW AGAINST THAT HOUSE.
AND IT ALL FELL DOWN AND ITS COLLAPSE WAS COMPLETE."

Inspired by Matthew 7:28-29

AND SO IT CAME ABOUT, AS JESUS FINISHED SPEAKING,
  THAT THE MULTITUDES OF PEOPLE
    WERE AMAZED BY HIS TEACHING.
FOR HE DID NOT PREACH AT THEM
  LIKE THEIR RELIGIOUS EXPERTS,
    BUT RATHER SPOKE TO THEM AS ONE WHO HAS AUTHORITY.

The Sabbath:
a Day in the
Life of Christ

from Mark 2:23-5:43

SUNRISE: The Synagogue

•⎯⎯⎯

Inspired by Mark 2:23-28

AND JESUS ARRIVED ON THE SABBATH DAY,
 GOING THROUGH FIELDS OF WHEAT.
AND HIS DISCIPLES CAME ALONG
 AND PROCEEDED TO PLUCK HEADS OF GRAIN TO EAT.
NOW, THE PHARISEES SAID TO HIM,
 "SEE HERE!
 WHY ARE THEY DOING WORK THAT IS
  NOT PERMISSABLE ON THE SABBATH?"
AND JESUS SAID TO THEM,
 "DON'T YOU RECALL WHAT DAVID DID,
  WHEN HE WAS DESPERATE AND HUNGRY?
   AND FOR THOSE WHO FOLLOWED HIM?
 WHEN ABIATHUR WAS HIGH PRIEST,
  HOW WAS IT RIGHT FOR DAVID
   TO ENTER THE HOUSE OF GOD
    AND EAT THE CONSECRATED BREAD
   WHICH NO ONE BUT THE HIGH PRIEST
   IS PERMITTED TO EAT?
 YET HE ATE IT,
  AS WELL AS THOSE WHO FOLLOWED HIM."
AND HE SAID TO THEM ALL,
 "THE SABBATH WAS CREATED
  FOR THE SAKE OF HUMANITY
 AND NOT HUMANITY
  FOR THE SAKE OF THE SABBATH –
 THEREFORE,
  THE ONE WHO IS THE SON OF MAN,
   THE TRUE HEIR OF HUMANITY,
  IS ALSO THE LORD OF THE SABBATH,
   THE DAY FOR REMEMBERING
    THE MULTITUDES OF CREATION."

Inspired by Mark 3:1-6

AND SO,

      JESUS WENT INSIDE THE SYNAGOGUE AT CAPERNAUM.

NOW, A MAN WITH AN UNDEVELOPED HAND WAS THERE –

      AND THEY WAITED TO SEE IF JESUS

          WOULD HEAL HIM ON THE SABBATH,

      SO THAT THEY COULD BRING CHARGES AGAINST HIM.

AND HE SAID TO THE MAN WITH THE UNFORMED HAND,

      "STAND IN OUR MIDST."

THEN, HE SAID TO THEM ALL,

      "IS IT 'PERMISSIBLE ON THE SABBATH'

          TO DO SOMETHING NICE

              OR TO DO SOMETHING EVIL?

          TO SAVE A LIFE OR TAKE ONE?"

      BUT THEY FESTERED IN SILENCE.

AND HE LOOKED AROUND AT THEM,

      BITTERLY GRIEVED AT THE INTRANSIGENT

          HARDNESS OF THEIR HEARTS.

HE SAID TO THE MAN,

      "STRETCH OUT YOUR HAND."

SO, HE STRETCHED IT OUT –

      AND HIS HAND WAS RE-GENERATED!

AND IMMEDIATELY, THE PHARISEES WENT OUT

      TO CONSULT WITH THE BUREAUCRAT HERODIANS

          AND <u>WORK</u> ON …

      HOW THEY WOULD DESTROY JESUS.

Inspired by Mark 3:7-12

AND JESUS WALKED OVER TO THE GALILEAN SEA,
  WITH HIS FRIENDS AND A HUGE CROWD.
THEY HAD COME FROM GALILEE AND JUDEA,
  FROM JERUSALEM AND IDUMAEA,
   FROM BEYOND THE JORDAN
  AND THE REGION AROUND TYRE AND SIDON!
THEY WERE A MULTITUDE OF MANY PEOPLE
  WHO HAD COME JUST BECAUSE THEY HAD HEARD ABOUT
   WHAT JESUS HAD BEEN DOING.

AND HE TOLD HIS FRIENDS TO SET A BOAT ASIDE
  FOR HIM TO GET INTO SO THAT THE CROWD
   WOULDN'T CRUSH HIM.
FOR MANY HAD COME TO BE HEALED
  AND HE WAS ABLE TO RELIEVE
   A GREAT DEAL OF SUFFERING.

THEN, A MAN WITH AN EVIL SPIRIT WAS HEALED,
  FALLING DOWN BEFORE JESUS
   AND SHREIKING AS IT WAS UPROOTED,
  "YOU ARE THE SON OF … !"
BUT JESUS FIRMLY REPRIMANDED ANY SUCH SPIRIT
  FROM ANNOUNCING WHAT HE WAS DOING!

MORNING: The Mountain

○ ─────────

Inspired by Mark 3:13-19

THEN, JESUS CLIMBED UP A HILL AND CALLED
        FOR SOME OF THEM TO APPROACH.
                SO, THEY WENT UP TO JESUS.
AND THERE, HE FORMED A GROUP OF TWELVE –
        WHOM HE APPOINTED AS MISSIONARIES,
                SO THAT, AS HIS COMPANIONS,
        HE WOULD SEND THEM OUT TO PREACH
                WITH THE POWER TO CAST OUT DEVILS.
THUS, JESUS CREATED 'THE TWELVE'
        AND HE LAID HIS HANDS UPON THEM, NAMING THEM:
                SIMON PETER 'THE ROCK',
        JAKE ZEBEDEESON AND HIS BROTHER JOHN,
                SURNAMED 'THUNDER' AND 'LIGHTNING',
        AND THERE WAS ANDREW,
                PHILLIP AND BARTHOLOMEW,
        MATTHEW AND THOMAS, JAKE ALFAEUSON,
                THADDEUS, SIMON 'THE PATRIOT',
                        AND JUDAS 'THE DAGGER' –
                WHO WOULD EVENTUALLY BETRAY JESUS.

NOON: The Street

○

———————

Inspired by Mark 3:20-27

AND THEY CAME BACK TO HIS MOTHER'S HOUSE,
    BUT THERE WAS SUCH A THRONG GATHERED THERE,
        THAT THEY COULDN'T GET IN FOR LUNCH.
MEANWHILE INSIDE THE HOUSE,
    MARY AND JESUS' BROTHERS & SISTERS
        HEARD A TERRIBLE COMMOTION –
SO THEY WENT OUTSIDE TO RESTRAIN JESUS,
        BECAUSE IT SOUNDED LIKE HE WAS
            GOING OUT OF HIS MIND WITH RAGE...

AND THE RELIGIOUS EXPERTS FROM JERUSALEM
    TAUNTED HIM, SAYING,
    "IT IS BY THE 'LORD OF THE FLIES'
        AND THE CHIEF OF THE DEVILS THAT YOU
        CAST OUT DEMONS!"
AND HE COUNTERED THEM WITH PARABLES,
    SAYING TO THEM,
    "HOW <u>WOULD</u> SATAN,
        CAST ITSELF OUT?
LIKE A THRONE DIVIDED,
        WOULD IT NOT COLLAPSE?
LIKE A HOUSE DIVIDED,
        WOULD IT NOT FALL DOWN?
THUS, SATAN DIVIDED
        WILL END WITH A CRASH.

    BUT NO ONE ENTERS A BULLY'S HOUSE,
        HIS GOODS TO TAKE.
YET FIRST, THIS BULLY
        BOUND I'LL MAKE.
SO THEN, THE GOODS GO FREE –
        AND IS IT NOT FOR <u>THEIR</u> SAKE?"

Inspired by Mark 3:28-35

[THEN 'THEY' SAID,
    "IT IS HE WHO HAS THE EVIL SPIRIT!"
AND BECAUSE OF THIS, JESUS WAS FURIOUS,]
    "I AM TELLING YOU <u>THE TRUTH</u>!!!
    <u>ALL</u> THE SINS AND CURSES
        COMMITED BY HUMANITY WILL BE FORGIVEN.
    BUT MISREPRESENTING GOOD BY CALLING IT EVIL
        IS TO BE BLIND TO THE SPIRIT OF WHAT IS GOOD!
    AND <u>THAT</u> CANNOT BE UNDONE BY ANYONE
        EXCEPT ONESELF…"

WHEN HIS MOTHER AND FAMILY HAD FINALLY ARRIVED,
    THEY WERE CALLING OUT FOR HIM TO STOP,
        BUT HE WAS SURROUNDED BY A CROWD.
AND SOMEONE SAID TO HIM,
    "LOOK OVER THERE!
    YOUR MOTHER AND YOUR BROTHERS AND SISTERS
        ARE WAITING FOR YOU!"
AND HE ANSWERED THEM, SAYING,
    "<u>WHO</u> ARE MY MOTHER
        AND MY BROTHERS AND SISTERS?"
THEN LOOKING AROUND AT THOSE GATHERED ABOUT,
    HE SAID,
    "<u>HERE</u> ARE
        MY 'MOTHER' AND 'BROTHERS' AND 'SISTERS'!
    ANYONE WHO DOES THE WILL OF GOD,
        WHICH IS SIMPLY TO LOVE,
    IS <u>MY</u> 'MOTHER'… AND <u>MY</u> 'BROTHER' AND <u>MY</u> 'SISTER.'"

AFTERNOON: The Beach

○

Inspired by Mark 4:1-10

AND JESUS WALKED BACK
    TO TEACH BESIDE THE SEA.
AS A GREAT CROWD GATHERED BEFORE HIM,
    HE GOT INTO A BOAT JUST OFFSHORE
        TO SIT DOWN WHILE ALL THE PEOPLE
    REMAINED ON THE BEACH.
AND HE TAUGHT THEM THROUGH MANY PARABLES
    AND IN HIS TEACHING, HE SAID,
    "LISTEN…IMAGINE…
    A FARMER WENT OUT TO SOW
        AND WHILE CASTING SEEDS,
            SOME FELL ALONG THE STREET.
        BUT BIRDS CAME AND ATE THEM UP.
    THEN OTHER SEEDS FELL ON ROCKY GROUND
        WHERE THERE WAS NOT A LOT OF DIRT.
            AND SOON AFTER, THEY SPRANG UP
                DESPITE THE SHALLOW SOIL.
            BUT WITH THE RISING OF THE SUN,
                THEY WERE SCORCHED.
            SO, HAVING NO DEEP ROOTS,
                THEY WITHERED AWAY.
    THEN OTHER SEEDS FELL AMONG THE BRAMBLES
        WHERE THE THORNS THRIVED
            BUT THESE SEEDS YIELDED NO GRAIN.
    AT LAST,
        SOME SEEDS FELL INTO THE PREPARED GROUND
            WHERE THEY GREW UP AND YIELDED GRAIN
        30 TIMES, 60 TIMES, EVEN UP TO 100 TIMES
            AS MUCH AS WAS PLANTED."
AND JESUS SAID,
    "WHOEVER HAS EARS THAT CAN HEAR,
        HAD BETTER BE LISTENING…"

AND THUS HE BEGAN TO ANSWER THOSE WHO
    CAME BEFORE HIM WITH QUESTIONS,
        TEACHING THEM ONLY WITH PARABLES.

Inspired by Mark 4:11-19

THEN HE SAID TO 'THE TWELVE'
        "TO YOU, THE MYSTERIES OF THE KINGDOM OF GOD,
                THE BELOVED COMMUNITY ARE REVEALED,
        BUT TO OUTSIDERS, IT WILL BE JUST STORYTELLING –
                [IT WILL BE LIKE RAP MUSIC].
        THEY WILL LOOK AND LOOK, BUT NOT SEE.
                THEY WILL LISTEN AND LISTEN, BUT NOT HEAR…
        UNLESS THEY TURN THEMSELVES AROUND –
                UNLESS THEY CULTIVATE THEIR HEARTS
EVEN TO BECOME ABLE
                TO FORGIVE AND ACCEPT FORGIVENESS."
AND HE DIDN'T SAY ANYTHING TO ANYONE
        THAT WASN'T A PARABLE.
BUT TO THE TWELVE, HE EXPLAINED
        HOW THESE STORIES WERE TO BE UNDERSTOOD…

        "THE WORD OF GOD IS THE SEED
                THAT IS SOWN.
        SO THIS IS LIKE THE WORD THAT IS SPREAD
                ALONG THE STREET.
        BUT WHEN HEARTS THAT ARE STREET-WISE HEAR IT,
                THE ENEMY IMMEDIATELY SNATCHES THE WORD
                        THAT WAS SOWN IN THEM.
        WHEN THE WORD HAS BEEN CAST
                UPON HEARTS LIKE ROCKY GROUND,
                        THEY INITIALLY GRASP IT WITH JOY.
                BUT HAVING NO 'ROOTS' WITHIN THEMSELVES,
                        IT IS TEMPORARY FOR THEM.
        THEREFORE, WHEN OPPRESSION AND PERSECUTION
                ARISES AGAINST THE WORD,
                        THEY FOLD TO TEMPTATION.
        WHEN THE WORD HAS BEEN CAST
                UPON HEARTS OVERGROWN WITH BRAMBLES,
                        THEY HEAR IT.
                BUT THEY ARE ALWAYS ANXIOUS FOR SECURITY
                        AND DECEIVED BY WEALTH,
                                WANTING MORE.
                AND THEIR LUST CROWDS THE WORD
                        SO THAT IT YIELDS NO 'GRAIN'."

Inspired by Mark 4:20-23

[THEN JESUS SAID,]

"AND LIKE SEEDS SOWN INTO GOOD SOIL
THAT PRODUCE A CROP,
SO ARE THEY WHO HEAR THE WORD OF GOD
AND YIELD 30 TIMES AND 60 TIMES
AND 100 TIMES AS MANY LIVES
THAT ARE SAVED."

AND HE SAID TO THEM,
"WOULD ANYONE SEEK THE LIGHT
IF THE LAMP WAS UNDER A BASKET?
WOULDN'T IT BE BETTER
IF THE LAMP WAS ON ITS STAND?

"BUT EVEN THOUGH THINGS ARE HIDDEN,
THEY WILL BE REVEALED.
EVEN THOUGH SECRETS ARE WHISPERED,
THEY WILL BE SHARED.

"WHOEVER HAS EARS THAT CAN HEAR,
HAD BETTER BE LISTENING…"

Inspired by Mark 4:24-34

AND JESUS SAID TO THEM,
 "LOOK AND LISTEN!
 THE MANEUVER ROOM YOU GIVE
  WILL BE THE SAME YOU GET.
 SO THOSE WHO ARE GENEROUS,
  WILL GET MORE THAN THEY GIVE.
 BUT THOSE WHO ARE STINGY
  WILL LOSE WHAT THEY GOT."
AND HE SAID,
 "THE KINGDOM OF GOD, THE BELOVED COMMUNITY,
  IS LIKE A FARMER WHO CASTS
   SEED UPON THE EARTH.
 AND WHILE THE FARMER SLEEPS THROUGH THE NIGHT
  AND AWAKENS TO THE DAY,
   THE SEED HAS SPROUTED AND IS GROWING,
  THOUGH THE SOWER DOES NOT KNOW HOW.
 THE GROUND ITSELF BRINGS FORTH THE PLANT,
  FIRST THE SHOOT, THEN THE GRAIN,
   FINALLY THE RIPENED HEAD OF WHEAT.
 AND WHEN THE CROP IS READY, RIGHT THEN,
  THE FARMER PASSES THROUGH THE FIELD
   TO BRING IN THE HARVEST."
AND HE SAID,
 "THE KINGDOM OF GOD, THE BELOVED COMMUNITY,
  CANNOT REALLY BE COMPARED TO ANYTHING,
   EXCEPT BY USING SIMPLE PARABLES.
 THOUGH THE MUSTARD SEED
  IS THE SMALLEST SEED ON EARTH,
   YET WHEN PLANTED,
  BECOMES THE LARGEST PLANT IN A GARDEN.
 THEN, EVEN THE BIRDS OF THE SKY
  SEEK THE SHADE BENEATH ITS BRANCHES
  JUST AS IT IS WITH BELOVED COMMUNITY."

AND WITH MANY PARABLES OF THIS KIND,
 HE ENTERTAINED THE PEOPLE,
  BUT FOR REVEALING THEIR MEANING,
 HE EXPLAINED EVERYTHING TO THE DISCIPLES.

Inspired by Mark 4:35-41

AND JESUS TOLD THE DISCIPLES THAT,
      "THOUGH THE DAY IS GROWING LATE,
            LET US CROSS OVER TO THE OTHER SIDE
              OF THE GALILEE."
AND LEAVING THE CROWD,
      THEY TOOK HIM ABOARD THEIR BOAT
            JUST AS HE WAS,
      AS OTHER BOATS ACCOMPANIED THEM.

THEN, A TEMPEST WAS FORMED BY STRONG WINDS
      AND SENT WAVES ROLLING OVER, INSIDE THE BOAT
            SO THAT IT WAS FLOODED!
BUT JESUS WAS IN THE STERN,
      ON THE CUSHION, EXHAUSTED.

AND THEY ROUSED HIM AND SAID TO HIM,
      "RABBI! TEACHER!
      DON'T YOU CARE THAT WE ARE SINKING?"
AND GETTING UP, HE SCOLDED THE WIND
      AND SAID TO THE SEA,
      "SILENCE! I SAY, BE SILENT!"
AND THE WIND DIED DOWN AND THE SEA BECAME CALM –
      AND BECAME THE GREAT, CALM GALILEE AGAIN.

AND HE SAID TO THEM,
      "WHY ARE YOU SO NERVOUS?
            DON'T YOU HAVE FAITH YET?"
BUT THEY WERE TERRIFIED WITH GREAT FEAR
      AND SAID TO ONE ANOTHER,
      "SO, WHO IS THIS REALLY
            THAT EVEN THE WIND AND THE SEA
            LISTEN UP TO HIM?"

MIDNIGHT: The Other Side

Inspired by Mark 5:1-10

AND THEY CAME TO THE OTHER SIDE OF THE SEA
     TO THE LAND OF THE GERASENES,
          'THE LAND OF THE PRIZE'.
SUDDENLY,
     AS JESUS WAS GETTING OUT OF THE BOAT,
          OUT FROM A GRAVEYARD CAME
     A MAN WITH A PERVERSE SPIRIT,
          RUNNING UP TO CONFRONT HIM!
THIS WAS SOMEONE WHO HAD BEEN LIVING IN THE GRAVEYARD,
     AND NOT EVEN CHAINS
          COULD HOLD HIM BACK ANYMORE
     NOR WAS THERE ANYONE WHO COULD.

DESPITE BEING FREQUENTLY SHACKLED,
     THE CHAINS WOULD GAVE WAY AND
          HE WOULD WRENCH THEM APART FROM HIS FEET.
AND NO ONE WAS STRONG ENOUGH
     TO SUBDUE HIM.
AND THROUGHOUT NIGHT AND DAY,
     IN THE TOMBS AND AMONG THE HILLS
          HE WOULD HOWL –
     AND HURT HIMSELF WITH ROCKS.
BUT WHEN HE SAW JESUS FROM A DISTANCE,
     HE CHARGED TOWARDS HIM…

[JESUS SAID,
     "YOU! EVIL SPIRIT!
     COME OUT OF THIS MAN!"]
AND THE MAN COLLAPSED BEFORE JESUS, GROVELING,
     "WHAT ARE YOU GOING TO DO TO ME,
          JESUS, SON OF THE HIGHEST GOD?
     I BEG YOU, DO NOT TORTURE ME!"
[JESUS QUESTIONED HIM,]
     "WHAT IS YOUR NAME?"
AND HE SAID,
     "MY NAME IS 'DIVISION' FOR WE ARE AN ARMY."
BUT HE URGED HIM DESPERATELY,
     "DON'T SEND ME OUT OF THIS REGION!"

Inspired by Mark 5: 11-20

NOW THERE WAS A HUGE HERD OF PIGS
     ROOTING ABOUT NEARBY, SO HE WHIMPERED,
     "SEND US TO THE PIGS SO THAT
        WE CAN ENTER THEM!"
BUT JESUS SENT THEM, "OUT!"
     YET THE EVIL SPIRIT CAME OUT –
        TO GO INTO THE PIGS.
THEN THE HERD RUSHED HEADLONG
     OVER THE STEEP CLIFF AND INTO THE SEA.
ABOUT 2,000 OF THEM WERE DROWNED
     IN THE WATERS.
AND THE SWINEHERDS FLED FROM THERE
     TO TELL EVERYONE IN THE TOWN
        AND THROUGHOUT THE COUNTRYSIDE.
SO, THE PEOPLE CAME TO LOOK AT WHAT HAD HAPPENED.

AS THEY APPROACHED JESUS,
     THEY NOTICED THAT THE ONE WHO
        HAD BEEN DEMON-POSSESSED,
     WAS SITTING CLOTHED AND COHERENT –
        THE 'DIVISION' WAS GONE.
BUT THEY BECAME SUSPICIOUS.

THEN, THE SWINEHERDS RECOUNTED WHAT THEY SAW
     HAPPEN WITH THE DEMON-POSSESSED MAN AND THE PIGS.
SO, THE PEOPLE APPEALED TO JESUS –
     TO LEAVE THEIR LAND.

AND AS JESUS WAS CLIMBING INTO THE BOAT,
     THE ONE WHO HAD BEEN POSSESSSED BY DEMONS
        ASKED JESUS,
     "LET ME JUST – BE WITH YOU."
BUT JESUS SAID TO HIM,
     "GO HOME TO YOUR LOVED ONES AND TELL THEM
        WHAT THE ONE WHO IS GOD HAS DONE
          AND HOW GOD HAS HAD MERCY UPON YOU."
SO, HE WENT HOME AND IN TIME, HE WENT FORTH,
     PROCLAIMING THROUGHOUT THE 10 CITIES
        OF THAT REGION ABOUT WHAT JESUS HAD DONE.
AND EVERYONE, EVERYWHERE WAS AMAZED WITH JOY.

FIRST LIGHT: The Return

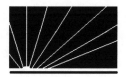

Inspired by Mark 5:21-30

AND CROSSING BY BOAT,

     JESUS CAME BACK TO THE JEWISH SIDE OF THE GALILEE.

THERE, GATHERED ON THE BEACH,

     WAS A HUGE CROWD WAITING FOR HIM...

AND THE MODERATOR OF THE CAPERNAUM SYNAGOGUE,

     NAMED JAIRUS, CAME UP TO HIM.

BUT LOOK HERE!

HE KNELT DOWN AT JESUS' FEET

     AND URGED HIM DESPERATELY, SAYING,

     "MY DAUGHTER IS IN THE FINAL STAGES OF DYING!

        COME, AND LAY YOUR HAND UPON HER

          SO THAT SHE CAN BE HEALED AND LIVE!"

SO, JESUS DEPARTED WITH HIM

     AND THIS HUGE CROWD ACCOMPANIED THEM,

     AND CLOSED IN AROUND HIM.

NOW, AMONG THEM WAS A WOMAN

     WITH A MENSTRUAL CONDITION.

FOR 12 YEARS, SHE HAD SUFFERED THROUGH

     THE TREATMENTS OF MANY PHYSICIANS,

        AND HAD SPENT HER WHEREWITHAL

     WITHOUT IMPROVEMENT, EVEN GROWING WORSE.

HAVING HEARD ABOUT JESUS,

     SHE APPROACHED HIM FROM BEHIND

        THROUGH THE CROWD

          JUST TO TOUCH HIS CLOTHES.

FOR SHE HAD SAID TO HERSELF,

     "IF I JUST TOUCH HIS CLOTHING, I WILL BE HEALED."

AND IMMEDIATELY,

     SHE WAS HEALED FROM THIS CONDITION

        AND <u>KNEW IT</u> BY HOW SHE FELT IN HER BODY.

AND IMMEDIATEDLY, JESUS <u>KNEW WITHIN HIMSELF</u>

     THAT ENERGY HAD GONE FORTH FROM HIM.

HE TURNED AROUND IN THE CROWD, SAYING,

     "WHO TOUCHED MY CLOTHES?"

Inspired by Mark 5:31-40b

AND THE DISCIPLES SAID TO HIM,
      "HA! YOU SEE THIS CROWD THRONGING ABOUT YOU,
            YET YOU SAY, 'WHO TOUCHED ME?' "
      BUT HE SEARCHED FOR THE ONE WHO DID THIS...

NOW, THE WOMAN WAS TERRIFIED AND TREMBLING,
      KNOWING WHAT HAD BEEN DONE WITHIN HER.
SHE CAME AND FELL DOWN BEFORE JESUS
      AND TOLD THE WHOLE TRUTH.
BUT JESUS SAID TO HER,
      "MY DEAR, MY DAUGHTER,
            YOUR FAITH HAS SAVED YOU!
      GO IN PEACE! SHALOM! SHALOM!
            AND BE SPARED FROM YOUR SUFFERING."

WHILE HE WAS STILL SPEAKING,
      SOMEONE CAME UP TO THE MODERATOR, SAYING,
      "YOUR DAUGHTER HAS PASSED AWAY!
            WHY TROUBLE THE RABBI AT THIS POINT?"
BUT IGNORING THIS,
      JESUS GAVE A WORD OF ENCOURAGEMENT,
            SAYING TO THE MODERATOR,
      "DON'T BE AFRAID – JUST TRUST ME."
AND HE DIDN'T ALLOW ANYONE GATHERED THERE
      TO GO WITH HIM EXCEPT PETER THE ROCK,
            JAKE, AND JAKE'S BROTHER JOHN.

AS THEY CAME TO THE MODERATOR'S HOUSE,
      THEY HEARD THE CLAMOR OF MANY PEOPLE,
            CRYING OUT AND LOUDLY WAILING.
AND AS HE ENTERED, JESUS SAID,
      "WHY DO YOU DISTRESS YOURSELVES AND WEEP?
            THE CHILD IS NOT DEAD – ONLY SLEEPING."
BUT THEY RIDICULED HIM,
      SO HE DROVE THEM ALL OUT!

Inspired by Mark 5:40b-43

JESUS TOOK ALONG THE FATHER OF THE CHILD –
    AND THE MOTHER…
        WHO WAS ALREADY AMONG THOSE WITH HIM!
    SO THEY ALL WENT IN TO WHERE THE CHILD WAS…

AND JESUS HELD THIS LITTLE ONE'S HAND,
    SAYING TO HER,
    "TALITHA, COUM!"
        WHICH IS TRANSLATED AS,
    "LITTLE GIRL, GET UP!"
AND IMMEDIATELY,
    THE LITTLE GIRL GOT UP
        AND STARTED RUNNING ALL AROUND!
    AFTER ALL SHE WAS 12 YEARS OLD.
AND IMMEDIATELY,
    THEY ALL WENT OUT OF THEIR MINDS
        WITH JOY,
    EVEN THOUGH JESUS WAS URGING THEM DESPERATELY,
    "DON'T SAY ANYTHING OF WHAT
        YOU KNOW ABOUT THIS!"
FINALLY, HE SAID,
    "OY! GIVE HER SOMETHING TO EAT."

a Lovesong to God

The Woman

Inspired by John 7:53-8:11

EVERYONE HAD GONE BACK TO THEIR OWN HOMES,
    EXCEPT JESUS.
HE WENT BACK TO THE MOUNT OF OLIVES –
    ALONE.
EARLY THE NEXT MORNING,
    HE AGAIN ENTERED THE TEMPLE.
WHEN THE WHOLE CONGREGATION
    WAS GATHERED BEFORE HIM,
        HE SEATED THEM TO INSTRUCT THEM.

THEN, THE PHARISEES AND RELIGIOUS EXPERTS
    BROUGHT IN A WOMAN CAUGHT IN ADULTERY.
AS SHE STOOD IN THEIR MIDST,
    THEY SAID TO HIM...
    "RABBI, TEACHER, THIS IS A WOMAN
        WHO WAS CAUGHT IN THE VERY ACT OF –
            WELL, SEXUAL MISCONDUCT.
    NOW IN OUR LAW, IT IS CLEAR:
        MOSES JUDGED THAT THIS SORT
            SHOULD BE STONED TO DEATH.
    WHAT DO YOU SAY ABOUT IT?"
NOW, THIS WAS SAID IN ORDER TO TEMPT JESUS
    INTO INDICTING HIMSELF.
INSTEAD, HE KNELT DOWN
    TO DRAW WITH HIS FINGER IN THE DIRT...

BUT AS THEY PERSISTED TO PROVOKE HIM,
    HE STOOD UP AND SAID TO THEM,
    "WHY NOT? BUT –
        LET SOMEONE WHO IS GUILTLESS AMONG YOU
            BE THE FIRST TO THROW A STONE AT HER."
AND HE SAT BACK DOWN
    TO DRAW ON THE GROUND...

YET, THOSE WHO UNDERSTOOD THIS
    DISPERSED ONE BY ONE,
        BEGINNING WITH THE ELDEST,
            OH... AND GOING AWAY SEPARATELY.

SO NOW, THE YOUNG WOMAN STOOD IN THE MIDST
OF NO ONE.
STANDING UP HIMSELF, JESUS SAID TO HER,
"YOUNG WOMAN, WHERE ARE THEY?
IS NO ONE GOING TO PUNISH YOU?"
SHE SAID,
"<u>NO</u> ONE…SIR!"
AND JESUS SAID,
"WELL, NEITHER WILL I PUNISH YOU.
YOU HAD BETTER GO.
BUT FROM NOW ON,
DO NOT DO WHAT IS HURTFUL TO YOU."

Inspired by Luke 7:36-8:2
JESUS WAS INVITED OVER TO EAT
     AT THE HOME OF A PHARISEE.
SO, HE ENTERED THE HOUSE
     AND RECLINED FOR DINNER.

NOW LOOK HERE!
A CERTAIN YOUNG WOMAN,
     WHO WAS KNOWN IN THE CITYFOR BEING A LOT OF TROUBLE,
          CAME INTO THE PHARISEE'S HOUSE AND
     SAT DOWN BEHIND JESUS, NEXT TO HIS FEET – WEEPING.
SHE HAD AN ALABASTER FLASK OF PERFUME
     WHICH SHE HAD BROKEN OPEN.
AND SHE DRIPPED SOME OF THE OIL ONTO HIS FEET –
     ALONG WITH HER TEARS.
SHE WIPED HIS FEET WITH HER HAIR AND KISSED THEM
     AS SHE RUBBED ON THE OIL.

BUT SEEING THIS, THE PHARISEE WHO HAD INVITED JESUS
     MUTTERED TO HIMSELF,
     "IF THIS FELLOW REALLY WERE A PROPHET,
          HE WOULD CERTAINLY KNOW WHO THIS IS.
     AND THAT THIS WOMAN WHO IS TOUCHING HIM
          HAS A REPUTATION."
AND JESUS ANSWERED HIM, SAYING,
     "SIMON, I HAVE SOMETHING TO SAY TO YOU."
HE SAID,
     "RABBI, SPEAK UP!"
JESUS SAID,
     "TWO DEBTORS WERE LOANED SOME MONEY:
          ONE BORROWED 500 DENARII
               AND THE OTHER 50,
          NEITHER COULD REPAY THE ONE
               WHO HAD LOANED THEM THE MONEY,
          BUT BOTH WERE FORGIVEN OF THEIR DEBTS.
     WHO WILL LOVE THE LENDER THE MORE?"

SIMON ANSWERED SAYING,
     "I SUPPOSE THE ONE WHO HAD BEEN
          FORGIVEN OF THE MOST."

AND JESUS SAID TO HIM,
     "YOUHAVE JUDGED CORRECTLY!"
THEN TURNING TO THE YOUNG WOMAN,
     HE SAID TO SIMON,
     "DO YOU SEE THIS GIRL?
          I CAME INTO YOUR HOUSE
          AND NO ONE GAVE ME WATER FOR MY FEET.
     BUT HER TEARS HAVE RAINED UPON MY FEET
          AND SHE HAS WIPED THEM WITH HER HAIR.
     NO ONE GREETED ME
          WITH A KISS,
     BUT SHE HAS NOT HELD BACK KISSES
          FOR MY FEET.
     NO ONE ANOINTED MY HEAD
          WITH OIL.
     BUT SHE HAS ANOINTED MY FEET
          WITH OIL.

     FORGIVENESS,
          I SAY TO YOU!
     HER SINS, EVEN THOUGH THEY WERE MANY,
          HAVE BEEN TAKEN AWAY
               BECAUSE OF HER GREAT LOVE.
     AH, BUT WHEN LITTLE GRIEF HAS BEEN TAKEN AWAY,
          IS THERE NOT LITTLE LOVE GIVEN IN RETURN?"
[IN OTHER VERSIONS OF THIS STORY,
     SIMON IS CALLED 'THE LEPER'.]

AND HE SAID TO THE YOUNG WOMAN,
     "YOUR SINS ARE FORGIVEN."

NOW, SOME OF THOSE WHO WERE SITTING THERE SAID,
     "WHO IS THIS?"
          "WHO CAN FORGIVE SINS?"

BUT JESUS SAID TO THE YOUNG WOMAN,
     "YOUR FAITH HAS SAVED YOU –
          YOU HAD BETTER GO.
               PEACE BE WITH YOU. SHALOM, SHALOM."

THEN, JESUS SET OUT FROM THERE,
    GOING FROM PLACE TO PLACE,
        ENTERING MANY CITIES AND VILLAGES,
    PROCLAIMING THE GOOD NEWS
        OF THE BELOVED COMMUNITY
            OF GOD'S KINGDOM.
AND THE TWELVE DISCIPLES WENT WITH HIM,
    AMONG THEM WOMEN,
        WHO HAD BEEN HEALED FROM EVIL SPIRITS
            AND OPPRESSION,
    INCLUDING MARY MAGDALENE
        FROM WHOM SEVEN DEVILS HAD BEEN
            DRIVEN AWAY...

Inspired by Luke 10:38-42

[out of sequence, but allows for a logical order of events that follow]

NOW IN THE COURSE OF HIS TRAVELS,
     JESUS ENTERED A PARTICULAR VILLAGE.
A WOMAN NAMED MARTHA WELCOMED HIM IN –
     WHOSE SISTER WAS MARY.
AND MARY SAT DOWN BESIDE THE FEET
     OF THE ONE WHO IS NOW CALLED 'THE LORD'
          TO LISTEN TO THE WORD OF GOD.
MEANWHILE, MARTHA WAS OVERWHELMED
     WITH MANY PREPARATIONS.
SO, JUSTIFIABLY, SHE SAID,
     "LORD, DON'T YOU CARE THAT,
          WHILE MY SISTER LEFT ME ALL ALONE,
               I AM STUCK WITH THE COOKING?
     TELL HER TO COME GIVE ME SOME HELP!"
BUT THE LORD ANSWERED HER, SAYING,
     "MARTHA, MARTHA!
     YOU ARE WORRIED AND DISTRESSED
          OVER AN EIGHT-COURSE BANQUET,
               WHEN ONE COURSE IS PLENTY FOR ME!
     BUT THE HEALTHY PORTION MARY IS BEING SERVED
     SHOULD NOT BE TAKEN AWAY FROM HER."

The Son of God

Inspired by Matthew 14:1-33

WHEN HEROD ANTIPAS THE POTENTATE
    HEARD ABOUT THE FAME OF JESUS,
        HE SAID TO HIS SERVANTS,
    "THIS IS JOHN THE BAPTIST!
        HE HAS BEEN RAISED FROM THE DEAD!
    THAT IS WHY THESE POWERS ARE AT WORK IN HIM!"

FOR HEROD HAD SEIZED JOHN AND PUT HIM IN PRISON
    ON ACCOUNT OF HIS BROTHER PHILLIP'S WIFE.
FOR JOHN HAD SAID TO HIM,
    "IT'S NOT LEGAL FOR YOU
        TO BE SLEEPING WITH HER!"
AND HEROD WOULD HAVE KILLED HIM FOR THIS,
    BUT HE WAS AFRAID OF THE PEOPLE
        BECAUSE THEY BELIEVED JOHN
        WAS A PROPHET…

BUT ON THE GALA OCCASION
    WHEN HEROD'S BIRTHDAY CAME,
        THE DAUGHTER OF HERODIAS BELLY-DANCED
        IN THE MIDST OF EVERONE.
AND HEROD WAS PLEASED, TO PUT IT POLITELY;
    SO MUCH SO, THAT HE SAID WITH AN OATH,
        THAT HE WOULD GIVE HER
    WHATEVER SHE MIGHT ASK FOR…

PROMPTED BY HER MOTHER,
    THE GIRL SAID,
    "GIVE ME THE HEAD OF JOHN THE BAPTIST –
        HERE ON A PLATTER!"

AND THE KING WAS SORRY,
    BUT BECAUSE OF HIS THOUGHTLESS OATHS
        AND HIS POWERFUL GUESTS,
    HE COMMANDED IT TO BE DONE.
AND SOMEONE WAS SENT
    TO DO IT.

JOHN WAS…
BEHEADED IN THE PRISON.
AND HIS HEAD WAS PLACED ON A PLATTER
AND PRESENTED TO THE GIRL –
AND SHE GAVE IT TO HER MOTHER!

WHEN JOHN'S DISCIPLES HEARD THIS,
THEY CAME AND TOOK HIS BODY
AND BURIED IT.
THEN, THEY REPORTED THIS TO JESUS.

AND WHEN JESUS HEARD THIS…
HE WENT AWAY FROM THERE,
SAILING IN A BOAT FOR A DESOLATE PLACE,
TO BE ALONE…TO PRAY.

BUT WHEN THE PEOPLE HEARD THIS,
THEY FOLLOWED AFTER HIM ON FOOT
FROM THE SURROUNDING TOWNS.

AS JESUS WAS GETTING OUT OF THE BOAT,
HE SAW A GREAT CROWD WAITING FOR HIM ON THE BEACH…
AND HE HAD COMPASSION ON THEM
AND HEALED THEIR SICK.

AS IT WAS GETTING LATE,
HIS DISCIPLES SAID TO HIM,
"THIS IS A DESOLATE PLACE
AND THE DAY IS ALMOST OVER.
SEND THE PEOPLE AWAY SO THAT
THEY CAN STILL GET TO THE VILLAGE
TO BUY FOOD FOR THEMSELVES."

BUT JESUS SAID TO THEM,
"THEY DON'T HAVE TO GO AWAY.
YOU GIVE THEM SOMETHING TO EAT!"
THEY SAID,
"WE HAVE NOTHING HERE! EXCEPT…
FIVE LOAVES OF BREAD AND TWO FISH."

JESUS SAID TO THEM,
        "BRING THEM HERE TO ME."
AND HE TOLD THE CROWDS,
        "SIT DOWN ON THE GRASS!"
THEN, HE TOOK THE FIVE LOAVES OF BREAD & TWO FISH
        AND BLESSED THEM AND BROKE THEM
                AND GAVE THEM TO THE DISCIPLES,
        WHO GAVE THEM TO THE CROWDS.

AND THEY ALL HAD SOMETHING TO EAT –
        AND THEY WERE SATISFIED!

AND THEY TOOK UP TWELVE BASKETS
        FULL OF BROKEN PIECES LEFT OVER.
NOW THOSE WHO ATE NUMBERED
        SOMETHING LIKE 5,000 MEN – THOUGH THEY NEGLECTED
                TO COUNT THE WOMEN & CHILDREN.

THEN SUDDENLY,
        JESUS URGED THE DISCIPLES TO BOARD THE BOAT
                AND GO AHEAD OF HIM
                        TO THE OPPOSITE SHORE,
        WHILE HE DISMISSED THE CROWDS.
AND WHEN HE HAD SENT THE CROWDS AWAY,
        HE WENT UP THE MOUNTAIN,
                TO BE ALONE, AT LAST TO PRAY.

MEANWHILE, THE BOAT WAS MANY LEAGUES OUT,
        BUT STILL FAR FROM LAND,
                BEING BATTERED BY WAVES
        CAUSED BY AN OPPOSING WIND.
[AND THE WORD FOR 'WIND' IN BOTH HEBREW AND GREEK
        CAN ALSO MEAN 'SPIRIT'.]
AND ABOUT FOUR O'CLOCK IN THE MORNING,
        SOMEONE WAS COMING TOWARDS THEM –
                WALKING ON THE SEA!
SO WHEN THE DISCIPLES SAW
        SOMEONE WALKING ON THE SEA,
                THEY WERE TERRIFIED, SAYING,

"IT'S A GHOST!"
        AND THEY HOWLED WITH FEAR.

BUT WHOEVER IT WAS CALLED BACK TO THEM,
        "HAVE COURAGE!
                I AM THE ONE WHO IS COMING TO YOU!
                DO NOT BE AFRAID!"

THEN, PETER THE ROCK ANSWERED HIM,
        "LORD – IF IT IS YOU,
                CALL FOR ME TO COME OUT TO YOU
                ON THE WATER!"
AND WHOEVER IT WAS SAID,
        "COME ON!"
AND HAVING CLIMBED OUT OF THE BOAT,
        PETER THE ROCK WAS WALKING ON THE WATER,
                AND CAME TO…
                JESUS!

BUT SEEING THE STRONG WIND,
        HE WAS AFRAID;
                AND BEGINNING TO SINK, HE CRIED OUT,
        "LORD, SAVE ME!"

INSTANTLY, JESUS REACHED OUT HIS HAND
        AND CAUGHT HIM.
AND HE SAID,
        "HAH! O BACKSLIDING BELIEVER…
                HOW COULD YOU DOUBT?"

AND AS THEY CLIMBED INTO THE BOAT;
        THE OPPOSING WIND CAME TO AN END…
IN THE BOAT,
        THEY KISSED HIS FEET, SAYING,
        "TRULY, YOU ARE THE SON OF GOD!"

The Samaritans

Inspired by Luke 9:51-62

NOW, IT WAS COMING ABOUT
　　　　THAT HIS DESTINY WOULD SOON BE FULFILLED:
　　　　　　　　THAT JESUS WOULD BE TAKEN UP INTO HEAVEN.
THEREFORE, HE SET HIS FACE TO GO TO JERUSALEM;
　　　　HE WAS DETERMINED TO CONFRONT JERUSALEM.

SO, HE SENT OUT MESSENGERS AHEAD OF HIM
　　　　AND THEY DEPARTED TO ENTER
　　　　　　　　A SAMARITAN VILLAGE IN ORDER TO
　　　　　　　　　　PREPARE FOR HIM.

HOWEVER, THESE SAMARITANS WERE NOT GOING TO
　　　　WELCOME HIM BECAUSE OF HIS PURPOSE:
　　　　　　　　TO GO TO JERUSALEM.
AND SEEING THIS, THE DISCIPLES JAMES AND JOHN,
　　　　'THUNDER' AND 'LIGHTNING' SAID,
　　　　"LORD, DO YOU WISH THAT FIRE BE COMMANDED
　　　　　　　　TO RAIN DOWN AND CONSUME THEM?"

BUT HE SPUN AROUND TO CONFRONT THEM,
　　　　"DON'T YOU KNOW WHAT SORT OF SPIRIT YOU ARE OF?
　　　　　　　　THE SON OF MAN, THE TRUE HEIR OF HUMANITY
　　　　　　　　　　DID NOT COME TO DESTROY HUMAN LIVES...
　　　　　　　　BUT TO SAVE THEM."
SO, THEY WENT SHEEPISHLY ALONG
　　　　TO THE NEXT VILLAGE.

AND AS THEY PROCEEDED ON THEIR JOURNEY,
　　　　SOMEONE SAID TO HIM,
　　　　"MAY I COME ALONG WITH YOU WHEREVER YOU GO?"
BUT JESUS SAID TO HIM,
　　　　"FOXES HAVE DENS TO LIVE IN
　　　　　　　　AND THE BIRDS OF THE SKY THEIR NESTS;
　　　　YET FOR THE SON OF MAN, THE HEIR OF HUMANITY,
　　　　　　　　THERE IS NOT EVEN A BED TO REST."

HOWEVER, JESUS SAID TO ANOTHER,
　　　　"COME ALONG WITH ME!"

AND THIS PERSON SAID,
 "LORD, ALLOW ME TO FIRST GO
  AND BURY MY FATHER."
BUT HE SAID,
 "SOMETIMES THE DEAD MUST BE ABANDONED
  TO BURY THEIR OWN DEAD.
 BUT AS FOR YOU… GO BACK.
  THEN, PROCLAIM THE BELOVED COMMUNITY
   OF GOD'S KINGDOM!"

STILL, ANOTHER SAID,
 "I WILL FOLLOW YOU, LORD.
  BUT FIRST, LET ME SAY GOODBYE TO MY FAMILY."
AND JESUS SAID TO HIM,
 "NO ONE WHO SETS HAND TO PLOW
  AND KEEPS LOOKING BACKWARDS
   CAN BE A RELIABLE FARMER!
 ALLOW YOURSELF TO <u>BE</u>
  IN THE BELOVED COMMUNITY
   OF GOD'S KINGDOM!"

Inspired by Luke 10:1-16

NOW, OF THOSE WHOM THE LORD WELCOMED,
    THERE WERE SEVENTY
        [PLUS THE TWO HE AT FIRST DISCOURAGED].
AND HE SENT THEM OUT TWO BY TWO AHEAD OF HIM
    INTO EVERY TOWN AND PLACE
        WHERE HE WAS DESTINED TO VISIT.

THEN, JESUS SAID TO THEM,
    "THOSE WHO ARE TO BE HARVESTED
        ARE ABUNDANT, BUT THE WORKERS ARE FEW.
PRAY, THEREFORE, THAT THE ONE WHO IS
    THE LORD OF THE HARVEST
WILL SEND OUT WORKERS TO DO THIS HARVESTING.

DO YOU SEE THAT YOU ARE BEING SENT OUT
    TO BE LAMBS AMIDST WOLVES?
DO NOT CARRY A MONEY BAG, A KNAPSACK,
    OR EXTRA SANDALS
AND DO NOT GET INVOLVED WITH THOSE
    YOU MEET ON THE ROAD…

BUT WHENEVER YOU COME TO A HOUSE, SAY,
    'SHALOM! PEACE BE UPON THIS HOME'.
AND IF THEY ARE CHILDREN OF PEACE,
    YOUR PEACE WILL STAY ON WITH THEM.
OTHERWISE, YOUR PEACE WILL JUST REMAIN
    WITH YOU.
IN ANY EVENT, STAY IN THE SAME HOUSE TO EAT AND DRINK,
    FOR A WORKER DESERVES TO BE PAID.
DO <u>NOT</u> GO FROM HOUSE TO HOUSE!

NOW, WHENEVER YOU COME TO A TOWN
    AND THEY WELCOME YOU,
        EAT WHATEVER THEY SET BEFORE YOU.
AND HEAL THEM IN THEIR DISTRESS AND TELL THEM,
    'THE BELOVED COMMUNITY OF GOD'S KINGDOM
        IS APPROACHING YOU!'

"BUT WHENEVER YOU COME TO A TOWN
        THAT DOES NOT WELCOME YOU,
                COME OUT BY THE ROADSIDE
        AND SAY THIS:
        'LIKE THE DIRT THAT CLINGS TO OUR FEET
                FROM YOUR TOWN,
                        WE SCRAPE OFF YOUR CONTEMPT!
        EVEN SO, KNOW THIS!
                'THE BELOVED COMMUNITY OF
                        GOD'S KINGDOM IS APPROACHING!'
I TELL YOU, WHEN THAT DAY COMES,
        IT WILL SEEM 'TOLERABLE'
                FOR SODOM AND GOMORRAH
        IN COMPARISON WITH WHAT IT WILL BE LIKE
                FOR THAT TOWN.

I GRIEVE FOR YOU, CHORAZIN!
        I GRIEVE FOR YOU, BETHSAIDA!
TYRE AND SIDON WOULD HAVE LONG AGO
        PUT ON HUMILITY AND KNELT
                IN REPENTANCE,
        IF THE POWERS GENERATED IN YOUR MIDST
                WERE PRODUCED AMONG THEM.
INDEED, IT WOULD BE 'BEARABLE'
        FOR TYRE AND SIDON COMPARED TO
                THE JUDGMENT THAT AWAITS YOU.
AND WHAT ABOUT YOU, CAPERNAUM!
        SHOULD YOU BE EXALTED UP TO HEAVEN?
                YOU WILL BE DUMPED INTO HELL, TOO!

THE ONE WHO LISTENS TO YOU, LISTENS TO ME
        AND THE ONE WHO REJECTS YOU, REJECTS ME;
                BUT THE ONE WHO REJECTS ME,
        REJECTS THE ONE WHO SENT ME."

Inspired by Luke 10:17-24

THEN, THE SEVENTY-TWO RETURNED JOYFULLY, SAYING,
>   "LORD! EVEN THE DEVILS NOW YIELD TO US
>   BECAUSE OF YOUR NAME!"
AND JESUS SAID TO THEM,
>   "I AM WATCHING AS SATAN, THE ENEMY OF HUMANITY,
>   IS BEING THROWN DOWN AS FAST AS
>   LIGHTNING FALLS FROM THE SKY!
>   LOOK HERE!
>   I HAVE GIVEN YOU THE MIGHT TO TRAMPLE
>   OVER SNAKES AND SCOPRPIONS
>   AND OVER ALL THE POWERS OF HATE;
>   AND ISN'T IT SO THAT
>   NONE OF YOU ARE HURT.
>   YET DO NOT REJOICE BECAUSE EVIL SPIRITS
>   YIELD TO YOU.
>   BUT REJOICE BECAUSE
>   YOUR NAMES ARE KNOWN IN THE HEAVENS!"

DURING THAT HOUR,
>   JESUS ENTERED INTO THE ECSTASY
>   OF THE HOLY SPIRIT,
>   THE LIFEBREATH OF HOLINESS, AND SAID,
>   "I PRAISE THEE, ABBA, FATHER,
>   LORD OF HEAVEN AND EARTH,
>   FOR CONFOUNDING THE STREETWISE & ARROGANT
>   WHILE UNVEILING THESE INNOCENT ONES.
>   YES, ABBA, FATHER!
>   THUS IN THIS WAY, GOODWILL WILL EMERGE
>   BEFORE THEE!

>   EVERYTHING HAS BEEN HANDED OVER TO ME
>   BY MY ABBA, MY HEAVENLY GUARDIAN;
>   AND NO ONE KNOWS WHO THE SON IS,
>   EXCEPT THE HEAVENLY GUARDIAN,
>   AND ONLY AS THE SON IS RESOLVED
>   TO BE REVEALED."

AND AS HE WAS TURNING TO THE DISCIPLES,
JESUS SAID, PARTLY TO HIMSELF,
"TO BE HONORED ARE THE EYES THAT SEE
WHAT THEIRS WILL SEE…

"FOR I SAY THIS BEFORE YOU BECAUSE
ALL PROPHETS AND KINGS DESIRED
TO SEE WHAT YOU SEE,
THOUGH NONE SAW;
AND TO HEAR WHAT YOU HEAR,
YET NONE OF THEM HEARD."

Inspired by Luke 10:25-37

NOW LOOK HERE!

A LAWYER GOT UP TO CHALLENGE HIM, SAYING,

"RABBI, TEACHER, WHAT MUST BE DONE

TO OBTAIN 'LIFE ETERNAL'?"

SO, JESUS SAID TO HIM,

"WHAT IS WRITTEN IN THE LAW?

HOW DO YOU INTERPRET IT?"

THEN, HE ANSWERED SAYING,

" 'YOU SHALL LOVE THE LORD YOUR GOD

WITH ALL YOUR HEART AND SOUL

AND WITH ALL YOUR MIGHT AND MIND.'

AND YOU SHALL LOVE YOUR NEIGHBOR

AS BEING LIKE YOURSELF –

AS BEING KIN, AS BEING FAMILY."

SO, JESUS SAID TO HIM,

"THAT'S THE RIGHT ANSWER.

DO THIS AND YOU WILL TRULY BE ALIVE!"

BUT WANTING TO MAKE HIS POINT,

THIS FELLOW SAID TO JESUS,

"SO, WHO IS MY 'NEIGHBOR'?"

PICKING UP ON THIS OPPORTUNITY, JESUS SAID,

"THERE WAS A MAN WHO WAS COMING DOWN

FROM JERUSALEM TO JERICHO

WHEN HE WAS AMBUSHED BY THIEVES.

AND THEY PLUNDERED HIM OF EVERYTHING

AND BRUTALLY BEAT HIM,

LEAVING HIM TO DIE.

BUT BY CHANCE,

A PRIEST WAS COMING DOWN THIS ROAD;

YET WHEN HE LOOKED AT THE MAN,

HE CROSSED AROUND HIM TO THE OTHER SIDE.

AND ONCE AGAIN, A RELIGIOUS PERSON

WAS COMING DOWN THE ROAD

BUT WHEN HE LOOKED AT THE MAN,

HE JUST CROSSED AROUND HIM, TOO.

"THEN, A SAMARITAN, WHO HAPPENED TO BE
TRAVELING THROUGH THERE,
APPROACHED HIM..
BUT HE SAW THIS PERSON
THROUGH THE EYES OF COMPASSION
AND HAD MERCY UPON HIM.
THIS FELLOW DRESSED UP THE MAN'S WOUNDS
BY POURING ON OIL, FLOUR, AND WINE.
THEN, HE PLACED THE MAN ON HIS OWN DONKEY,
AND LED HIM TO AN INN,
WHERE HE TOOK CARE OF HIM.
AND THE NEXT DAY,
HE TOOK OUT TWO DENARII, ABOUT $40,
TO GIVE TO THE INNKEEPER, AND SAID,
'TAKE CARE OF HIM AND WHATEVER
YOU SPEND IN ADDITION TO THIS,
I WILL REPAY YOUR ADVANCE TO ME
UPON MY RETURN.'

WHICH OF THESE THREE, DO YOU SUPPOSE,
BECAME A NEIGHBOR TO THE ONE
WHO HAD BEEN MUGGED BY THE THIEVES?"

AND THE LAWYER SAID,
"THE ONE WHO HAD ACTED MERCIFULLY TO HIM."
THEN, JESUS SAID TO HIM,
"GO AND YOU DO THE SAME."

The Son of Man

Jesus @ 2000

Inspired by John 11:1-57

THEN, A CERTAIN PERSON WAS STRICKEN ILL.
    IT WAS LAZARUS OF BETHANY, THE VILLAGE OF MARY
        AND HER SISTER, MARTHA.
INDEED, IT WAS THIS SAME MARY,
    WHO HAD ANOINTED THE LORD WITH OIL,
        AND DRIED HIS FEET WITH HER HAIR –
WHOSE BROTHER WAS LAZARUS!

SO, MARY SENT A MESSAGE TRO JESUS SAYING,
    "LORD, ONE WHO IS YOUR BELOVED FRIEND
        IS DEATHLY SICK."
BUT AFTER HEARING THIS, JESUS SAID,
    "THIS SICKNESS WILL NOT LEAD TO DEATH,
        BUT IT IS FOR THE SAKE OF GOD'S BLESSING
    THAT THE SON OF GOD WILL BE
        BLESSED THROUGH HIM.

SO, EVEN THOUGH HE KNEW THIS WAS AN EMERGENCY,
    JESUS STAYED WHERE HE WAS FOR TWO DAYS.
AFTERWARDS, HE SAID TO THE DISCIPLES,
    "LET'S GO BACK TO JUDEA."
THE DISCIPLES SAID TO HIM,
    "RABBI, LATELY THE JUDEANS HAVE BEEN
        OUT TO STONE YOU!
            AND YOU WANT TO GO BACK THERE AGAIN?"

JESUS ANSWERED,
    "ARE THERE NOT TWELVE HOURS OF DAYLIGHT
        WHEN ANYONE CAN GO ABOUT
        THROUGH THE DAY
        WITHOUT BUMPING INTO SOMETHING
        BECAUSE THEY SEE
            BY THE LIGHT OF THIS WORLD?

"BUT WHEN SOMEONE GOES ABOUT AT NIGHT,
    THEY BUMP INTO THINGS
        IF THEY HAVE NO LIGHT WITH THEM…

LAZARUS, OUR DEAR FRIEND, HAS FALLEN ASLEEP
        SO I AM GOING TO AWAKEN HIM."
THEN THE DISCIPLES SAID,
        "LORD, IF HE HAS ONLY FALLEN ASLEEP,
                HE WILL BE ALRIGHT."

BUT JESUS WAS TALKING ABOUT THE DEATH OF LAZARUS;
        SO AS TO ENLIGHTEN THEM ABOUT
                THIS 'FALLING TO SLEEP',
                        HE SPOKE ABOUT SLEEP,
        BUT NOW HE TOLD THEM BLUNTLY,
        "LAZARUS IS DEAD!
                AND I HOPE YOU WILL COME TO BELIEVE
                        BECAUSE WE WERE NOT THERE.
        BUT NO MATTER WHAT,
                I AM GOING TO HIM!"
THEN, THOMAS, THE ONE CALLED 'THE TWIN',
        SAID TO HIS FELLOW DISCIPLES,
        "LET'S ALSO GO AND DIE WITH HIM!"

JESUS CAME TO FIND THAT LAZARUS WAS ALREADY
        IN THE TOMB FOR FOUR DAYS.
NOW, BETHANY IS NEAR JERUSALEM,
        ABOUT TWO MILES AWAY;
                SO, MANY JUDEANS HAD COME IN ORDER TO
        CONSOLE MARTHA AND MARY
                ABOUT THEIR BROTHER.
AND AFTER HEARING THAT JESUS HAD ARRIVED,
        MARTHA WENT OUT TO MEET HIM –
                BUT MARY STAYED HOME…

MEANWHILE, MARTHA CONFRONTED JESUS, SAYING,
        "LORD, IF YOU HAD BEEN HERE
                MY BROTHER WOULD NOT HAVE DIED –
        BECAUSE I KNOW THAT WHATEVER
                WOULD HAVE BEEN ASKED OF GOD,
                        GOD WOULD HAVE GIVEN YOU!"
JESUS SAID TO HER,
        "I WILL RAISE UP YOUR BROTHER!"

MARTHA SAID TO HIM,
"I KNOW THAT THERE WILL BE A 'RAISING UP'
        IN THE RESURRECTION AT THE END OF TIME…"
JESUS SAID TO HER,
        "I AM THE ONE WHO RAISES UP
            AND THE ONE WHO GIVES LIFE.
        THOSE WHO TRUST ME WILL NOT BE DISAPPOINTED
            AND THOSE WHO LIVE TRUSTING IN ME
                WILL NOT DIE IN THE TIME TO COME.
        DO YOU BELIEVE THIS?"
SHE SAID TO HIM,
        "YES, LORD, I BELIEVE THAT YOU ARE THE MESSIAH,
            THE ONE WHO DESCENDED FROM GOD,
        THE ONE WHO IS PROCEEDING INTO THE WORLD!"

AND HAVING SAID THIS, SHE DEPARTED AND
        SPOKE PRIVATELY WITH HER SISTER, MARY, SAYING,
        "THE RABBI, THE TEACHER, IS HERE
            AND…HE NEEDS YOU!"
UPON HEARING THIS,
        SHE GOT UP QUICKLY AND WENT OUT TO HIM.
WHEN THE JUDEANS,
        WHO WERE GRIEVING WITH MARY IN THE HOUSE,
            SAW HER GET UP QUICKLY AND GO OUT,
        THEY SUPPOSED THAT SHE WAS GOING TO THE TOMB
            TO MOURN THERE – SO THEY FOLLOWED …

NOW, JESUS HAD NOT YET ENTERED THE VILLAGE,
        BUT WAS STILL ON THE HILL WHERE
            MARTHA HAD MET HIM.
WHEN MARY CAME TO THE PLACE WHERE JESUS WAS,
        SHE LOOKED AT HIM …
            AND KNELT DOWN BEFORE HIM, SAYING,
        "LORD, IF YOU HAD BEEN HERE
            MY BROTHER WOULD NOT HAVE DIED."
WHEN JESUS SAW HER CRYING AND THOSE JUDEANS
        WHO HAD COME WITH HER ALSO CRYING,
            HE WAS OVERWHELMED IN THE SPIRIT –
HE, HIMSELF, WAS DEEPLY MOVED!

AND HE SAID,
    "WHERE DID YOU LAY HIM DOWN?"
THEY SAID TO HIM,
    "LORD, COME AND SEE. FOR YOURSELF."
JESUS BURST INTO TEARS.

THEN, THE JUDEANS SAID,
    "DO YOU SEE HOW HE LOVED HIM?"
STILL SOMEONE SAID,
    "COULD NOT THIS FELLOW,
        WHO OPENED THE EYES OF BLIND PEOPLE,
    THEREFORE BE ABLE
        TO RAISE UP THIS PERSON, TOO?"

AS HE APPROACHED THE TOMB,
    AGAIN JESUS WAS OVERWHELMED WITH EMOTION.
NOW, THE TOMB WAS COVERED WITH A ROCK UPON IT,
    AND JESUS SAID,
    "SOMEONE LIFT UP THE ROCK."
BUT MARTHA, THE SISTER OF THE ONE WHO HAD DIED,
    SAID,
    "LORD, THERE WILL BE CORRUPTION,
        BECAUSE IT HAS BEEN FOUR DAYS!"
JESUS SAID TO HER,
    "DIDN'T I SAY TO YOU THAT YOU WOULD SEE
        GOD'S BLESSING IF YOU TRUST ME?"
SO, THE ROCK WAS LIFTED UP.

AND JESUS LIFTED UP HIS EYES TO HEAVEN AND SAID,
    "I THANK THEE ABBA, FATHER,
        FOR LISTENING TO ME.
    NOW, I KNOW THAT THOU HEAR ME ALWAYS!
        BUT SPEAK THROUGH
            THIS CROWD STANDING ABOUT
        SO THAT THEY WILL KNOW
            THAT THOU SENT ME!"

HAVING SAID THIS, JESUS CRIED OUT IN A LOUD VOICE,
    "LAZARUS! COME OUT!"

[AND] THE ONE WHO HAD DIED CAME OUT,
    HIS HANDS AND FEET STILL TIED,
        HIS FACE WRAPPED IN A COVERING.
JESUS SAID TO THEM,
    "UNBIND HIM AND LET HIM GO!"

SO, ALL THE JUDEANS WHO CAME WITH MARY
    AND SAW WHAT HAPPENED, BELIEVED IN HIM.
STILL SOME WENT TO TELL THE PHARISEES –
    WHO GATHERED AT THE COUNCIL AND TALKED…
    "HOW IS IT THAT THIS FELLOW IS
        DOING ALL THESE WONDER-WORKS?"
IF WE PERMIT THIS TO GO ON,
        EVERYONE WILL CERTAINLY… WILL CERTAINLY…
        BELIEVE IN HIM!"
"AND THE ROMANS WILL BE UNLEASHED AGAINST US
    AND SWEEP US AWAY FROM OUR OWN LAND
        AS WELL AS OUR WAY OF LIFE!"

BUT ONE WHO WAS PROMINENT AMONG THEM – CAIAPHAS,
    WHO WAS HIGH-PRIEST THAT YEAR, SAID TO THEM,
    "YOU DO NOT UNDERSTAND ANY OF THIS AT ALL!
        YOU HAVE NOT REASONED AS TO HOW IT
            FITS TOGETHER FOR YOUR OWN PURPOSE:
        THAT ONE PERSON DIE
            FOR THE SAKE OF THE PEOPLE
        SO THAT THE WHOLE NATION
            WILL NOT BE DESTROYED."
NOW, HE DID NOT IMPART THIS AS HIS OWN OPINION,
    BUT AS 'HIGH-PRIEST OF THE YEAR' HE PROPHESIED
        THAT THIS WOULD CERTAINLY TAKE PLACE:
    "JESUS WILL DIE FOR THE NATION,
        YET NOT FOR THE NATION ALONE,
    BUT SO THAT ALL THE SCATTERED
        CHILDREN OF GOD
            WILL BE GATHERED TOGETHER IN UNITY!"

AND FROM THEN ON, THEY DELIBERATED
    AS TO HOW TO PUT JESUS TO DEATH.

SO, JESUS NO LONGER WENT ABOUT PUBLICLY
        AMONG THE JUDEANS,
                BUT RETREATED TOWARDS THE DESERT REGION
        TO STAY AT THE CITY OF EPHRAIM WITH HIS DISCIPLES.

BUT AS THE TIME FOR THE JEWISH PASSOVER DREW NEAR,
        MANY PEOPLE WERE GOING UP TO JERUSALEM
                FROM THE SURROUNDING REGIONS
                        TO SPIRITUALLY PREPARE THEMSELVES.
MEANWHILE, THOSE AT THE TEMPLE WERE
        GETTING ANXIOUS ABOUT JESUS
                AND ASKED EACH OTHER WITH MUTUAL CONCERN,
        "DON'T YOU THINK 'HE' WILL COME TO THE FESTIVAL?"
BUT THE HIGH-PRIESTS AND PHARISEES
        INSTRUCTED THEM ABOUT THE PURPOSE, PLACE,
                AND PREPARATIONS FOR SEIZING JESUS…

Inspired by John 19:25-30

NOW STANDING BESIDE THE CROSS OF JESUS
    WAS HIS MOTHER, HIS AUNT MARY THE WIFE OF CLEOPAS,
        AND MARY MAGDALENE.
THEN, JESUS SAW HIS MOTHER AND
    THE DISCIPLE WHO WAS HIS BELOVED FRIEND,
        STANDING TOGETHER.
HE SAID TO HIS MOTHER,
    "LOOK AFTER THIS ONE AS YOUR OWN CHILD."
AND THEN SAID TO THE DISCIPLE,
    "LOOK AFTER THIS ONE AS YOUR OWN MOTHER."
SO FROM THEN ON,
    SHE TREATED THAT DISCIPLE AS HER OWN CHILD.

WITH THAT, JESUS KNEW THAT ALL WAS ACCOMPLISHED;
    IN ORDER TO FULFILL THE SCRIPTURES, HE SAID,
    "I THIRST!"
THEY HAD A JUG FULL OF SOUR WINE THERE
    WHICH THEY SOAKED INTO A SPONGE
        AND TIED TO A JAVELIN.
THEY BROUGHT IT UP TO HIS MOUTH;
    AND WHEN HE HAD TAKEN THE WINE, JESUS SAID,
    "IT IS DONE!"
AND HE BOWED HIS HEAD
    AS HE RELEASED HIS SPIRIT.

NOW ON WHAT WOULD BECOME
    THE CHRISTIAN SABBATH DAY,
        MARY MAGDALENE CAME TO THE TOMB,
    EARLY IN THE MORNING
        WHILE IT WAS STILL IN GLOOM.
WHEN SHE SAW THAT THE ROCK
    HAD BEEN ROLLED AWAY FROM THE TOMB,
        SHE RAN…
[Verses 2b-12 about the "beloved disciple"– traditionally believed to be John, are omitted for poetic/prophetic license.]

John 20:11-18
LATER, MARY WAS STANDING OUTSIDE,
    IN FRONT OF THE TOMB, CRYING,
STILL WEEPING, SHE KNELT DOWN BY THE GRAVESIDE…
    AND SAW TWO ANGELIC BEINGS,
        CLOAKED IN RADIANCE,
    SEATED AT THE HEAD AND FOOT OF WHERE
        JESUS' BODY HAD BEEN!
AND THEY SAID TO HER,
    "YOUNG WOMAN, YOUNG WOMAN,
        WHY ARE YOU CRYING, WHY ARE YOU CRYING?"
SHE SAID TO THEM,
    "BECAUSE MY LORD HAS BEEN TAKEN AWAY
        AND I DO NOT KNOW
            WHERE HE HAS BEEN HIDDEN!"

SOMEONE WAS SPEAKING BEHIND HER;
    SHE TURNED AND LOOKED.
IT WAS JESUS STANDING THERE,
    BUT SHE DID NOT RECOGNIZE THAT IT WAS JESUS.
JESUS SAID TO HER,
    "YOUNG WOMAN, WHY ARE YOU CRYING?
        WHOM DO YOU SEEK?"
SUPPOSING THAT HE WAS THE GROUNDSKEEPER,
    SHE SAID TO HI M,
    "SIR, IF YOU HAVE TAKEN HIM, TELL ME WHERE
        YOU BURIED HIM AND I WILL CARE FOR HIM!"

HE SAID TO HER,
 "OH, MARY!"
SHE WHIRLED AROUND AND SAID TO HIM,
 "RABBOUNI!" – WHICH IN ARAMAIC MEANS,
  "MY DEAR RABBI!"

JESUS SAID TO HER,
 "OY! DON'T HOLD ME SO TIGHT!
  I STILL MUST GO UP TO HEAVEN!
 YOU HAD BETTER GO –
  AND TELL MY BROTHERS AND SISTERS
   THAT I AM GOING UP
    TO MY ABBA, MY FATHER,
  MY HEAVENLY GUARDIAN
   AND YOUR HEAVENLY GUARDIAN,
 TO MY GOD AND YOUR GOD!"

MARY MAGDALENE WENT FORTH FROM THERE
 TO PROCLAIM THIS TO THE APOSTLES:
 "I FOUND THE LORD
  AND HE SPOKE WITH ME!"

   [AND GOD IS STILL SPEAKING]

αμην
Amen